Universal credit
What you need to know

Child Poverty Action Group

Published by Child Poverty Action Group
30 Micawber Street
London N1 7TB
Tel: 020 7837 7979
info@cpag.org.uk
cpag.org.uk
© Child Poverty Action Group 2024

This book is sold subject to the condition that it shall not, by way of trade or otherwise, be lent, resold, hired out or otherwise circulated without the publisher's prior consent in any form of binding or cover other than that in which it is published and without a similar condition including this condition being imposed on the subsequent purchaser.
A CIP record for this book is available from the British Library.
ISBN: 978 1 915324 17 7

Child Poverty Action Group is a charity registered in England and Wales (registration number 294841) and in Scotland (registration number SC039339), and is a company limited by guarantee, registered in England (registration number 1993854). VAT number: 690 808117

Cover design by Colorido Studios
Internal design by Devious Designs
Typeset by DLxml, a division of RefineCatch Limited, Bungay, Suffolk
Content management system by KonnectSoft
Printed and bound in the UK by CPI Group (UK) Ltd, Croydon CR0 4YY

Authors
Simon Osborne is a welfare rights worker at CPAG.
Owen Polley is a welfare rights worker at CPAG.
Owen Stevens is a welfare rights worker at CPAG.

Acknowledgements
Thanks are due to the authors of the previous editions. Many thanks are due to Mark Willis and Dan Norris for efficient and thorough checking of this edition. Thanks also to Kathy Proctor for editing and managing the production, Katherine Dawson for producing the index and Kathleen Armstrong for proofreading the text.

About Child Poverty Action Group

Child Poverty Action Group (CPAG) is a national charity that works on behalf of the more than one in four children in the UK growing up in poverty. We use our understanding of what causes poverty and the impact it has on children's lives to campaign for policies that will prevent and solve poverty – for good.

We provide trusted and expert information and advice for the welfare rights and advice community – online, and through our books, training and advice services. Our advice lines support thousands of advisers a year, helping them to give families the best information and advice. Our *Welfare Benefits Handbook*, described as the 'adviser's bible', is used by Citizens Advice, local authorities and law centres throughout the UK. We also keep advisers up to date with trends and changes in the social security system through bulletins and our highly regarded training courses and seminars.

Poverty affects more than one in four children in the UK today. When children grow up poor they miss out – and so do the rest of us. They miss out on the things most children take for granted: warm clothes, school trips, having friends over for tea. They do less well at school and earn less as adults. Any family can fall on hard times and find it difficult to make ends meet. But poverty is not inevitable. With the right policies every child can have the opportunity to do well in life, and we all share the rewards of having a stronger economy and a healthier, fairer society. If you would like to join us to help end child poverty, please visit cpag.org.uk or follow us on Facebook (facebook.com/cpaguk) and X (@cpaguk).

Keeping up to date

You can get the latest information on benefits by booking on a CPAG training course. We can also provide your workplace with in-house training. Our training courses are currently available online, so you can attend from wherever you are working. See cpag.org.uk/training for more information.

Our *Welfare Benefits Handbook*, published every April, tells you all you need to know about entitlement to benefits. Visit cpag.org.uk/shop to purchase a copy.

With up-to-date information, insights, decision-making tools and appeal letter generators, CPAG Welfare Rights is our online platform that supplements the expertise advisers have come to trust and rely on from our rights handbooks and training. CPAG Welfare Rights provides digital access to our flagship *Welfare Benefits Handbook*, which is fully searchable and updated throughout the year online. See cpag.org.uk/subscriptions to subscribe or find out more.

Universal credit Early Warning System

CPAG's Early Warning System collects and analyses information about the impact of the roll-out of universal credit, as well as other changes in the benefits system. The cases we hear about inform our legal challenges, policy and campaign work. You can submit case studies or read our findings at cpag.org.uk/early-warning-system.

Getting advice

Your local Citizens Advice office or other advice centre can give you advice on benefits. See citizensadvice.org.uk and advicelocal.uk.

CPAG has a range of advice services for advisers.

For advisers in England, Wales and Northern Ireland:

Telephone: 020 7812 5231, Monday to Friday 10am to 12pm and 2pm to 4pm (for advice about any welfare benefit matter).

Email: advice@cpag.org.uk (for enquiries about universal credit and child benefit only).

Advisers supporting people living in London can get advice on universal credit by emailing UC-London@cpag.org.uk or by calling 020 7812 5221 (Wednesday 10am to 12pm and 2pm to 4pm).

For advisers in Scotland:

Telephone: 0141 552 0552, Monday to Thursday 10am to 4pm and Friday 10am to 12pm.

Email: advice@cpagscotland.org.uk.

For further information on CPAG's advice services, please visit cpag.org.uk/welfare-rights or cpag.org.uk/scotland/welfare-rights.

Contents

Chapter 1 **What is universal credit** 1

Chapter 2 **Transferring to universal credit** 6

Chapter 3 **Who can get universal credit** 18

Chapter 4 **Claiming universal credit** 30

Chapter 5 **The amount of universal credit** 48

Chapter 6 **Your responsibilities** 77

Chapter 7 **Sanctions, fines and fraud** 107

Chapter 8 **Overpayments** 121

Chapter 9 **Challenging a decision** 128

Chapter 10 **Universal credit and specific groups of people** 133

Appendix **Glossary of terms** 157

Index 167

Note:

Terms put in 'quotation marks', the first time they are used in a section, are defined in the Appendix (except in a few cases where they are explained in that same section).

Throughout the book, the Department for Work and Pensions is referred to as the DWP.

Chapter 1
What is universal credit

This chapter covers:

1. What is universal credit?
2. What is happening to the old benefits system?
3. How is universal credit administered?
4. How is universal credit different?

What you need to know

- Universal credit is a benefit for people of working age who are in or out of work.
- Universal credit is administered by the DWP and is claimed online.
- The amount of your universal credit depends on your income and savings – ie, it is 'means tested'. You do not need to have paid national insurance contributions to qualify.
- Claimants of the old means-tested benefits and tax credits have either already been transferred to universal credit by the DWP or will have been moved by the end of 2025, although this schedule might change.

1. What is universal credit?

Universal credit is a social security benefit for people of working age. It combines 'means-tested' support for adults, children and housing costs into one benefit.

The old means-tested benefits and tax credits for working-age people are being replaced by universal credit. This means that if you are, for example, a lone parent, sick or disabled, a carer, unemployed or in low-paid work, and you make a new claim for help with your living expenses, the means-tested benefit you will claim is universal credit.

2. What is happening to the old benefits system?

Working-age 'means-tested benefits' and tax credits are being replaced by universal credit. You cannot usually make a new claim for the benefits and tax credits listed in Box A. The DWP refers to these benefits and tax credits as 'legacy benefits'.

> Box A
> **Benefits and tax credits being replaced**
>
> The benefits and tax credits being replaced by universal credit are:
>
> - income support
> - income-based jobseeker's allowance
> - income-related employment and support allowance
> - housing benefit (with some exceptions)
> - child tax credit
> - working tax credit

If you are already getting one of these old benefits or tax credits, you can continue to do so until you claim, or are transferred to, universal credit. The main transfer process began in 2023 and is expected to be completed by the end of 2025, although there have been several delays and the end date may be subject to change. There is more information about transfers to universal credit in Chapter 2.

Universal credit does not replace all the current benefits. You can still claim, or continue to get, the benefits in Box B after universal credit has been introduced.

Box B
Which benefits remain?
- attendance allowance (or pension age disability payment in Scotland, when introduced)
- bereavement support payment
- carer's allowance (or carer support payment in Scotland)
- child benefit
- child winter heating assistance in Scotland
- cold weather payments and winter fuel payment (or winter heating payment in Scotland)
- constant attendance allowance
- contribution-based jobseeker's allowance
- contributory employment and support allowance
- disability living allowance for children (or child disability payment in Scotland)
- free school lunches
- funeral payments (or funeral support payment in Scotland)
- guardian's allowance
- Healthy Start vouchers (or Best Start foods in Scotland)
- help with health costs
- industrial injuries benefits (or employment injury assistance in Scotland, when introduced)
- maternity allowance
- pension credit
- personal independence payment (or adult disability payment in Scotland)
- state pension
- Scottish child payment in Scotland
- statutory adoption, maternity and paternity pay
- statutory shared parental pay and statutory shared parental bereavement pay
- statutory sick pay
- Sure Start maternity grant (or Best Start grant in Scotland)
- war disablement pension
- war widow's and widower's pension
- widowed parent's allowance

3. How is universal credit administered?

The **DWP** is responsible for the administration of universal credit. The DWP also deals with the old means-tested benefits that are being replaced and handles the transfer of these claims to universal credit.

HM Revenue and Customs (HMRC) administers tax credits, which are being replaced by universal credit. HMRC receives 'real-time information' on earnings from employers, which is then accessed by the DWP, so that universal credit payments can be automatically adjusted as people's earnings change.

Work coaches in local job centres oversee the 'work-related requirements' most people must meet in return for getting universal credit. There is more information about these in Chapter 6.

Citizens Advice has been funded by the government to provide a 'Help to Claim' universal support service.

4. How is universal credit different?

There are a number of differences between universal credit and the old benefits and tax credits system.

- **Monthly assessment and payment periods.** Universal credit is assessed according to your circumstances over a month. Awards are based on your earnings and other income received in a month, and payment is usually made in one monthly sum.

- **Online access.** Universal credit is claimed online. You manage your claim by signing into an online account. The DWP may allow telephone access in limited circumstances and assistance in person in exceptional cases. There is no paper claim form.

- **No hours rules.** The old system has a variety of rules on the number of hours you can work. These make a difference to your entitlement and the amount of benefit you receive, depending on whether you or your partner work less or more than 16, 24 or 30 hours a week. Under universal credit, all work is permitted, encouraged and, in some cases, required, and earnings are automatically taken into account. Universal credit is designed to allow people to work a few hours a week.

- **Work incentives.** Universal credit was first introduced with a defining principle of 'making work pay', with work incentives that allow claimants to keep more of their universal credit as their earnings rise. For most claimants, this now means being better off by 45 pence for every £1 they earn. Some claimants get a 'work allowance' – an amount they can earn before their benefit is reduced in this way.

- **In-work conditionality.** Universal credit claimants who work part time may be obliged to look for more work. This is not a feature of the old working tax credit system, in which you can qualify if you work a certain number of hours. Universal credit claimants who do not do enough to increase their hours or pay can be given a 'sanction' (and the amount of their benefit is reduced).

Chapter 2
Transferring to universal credit

This chapter covers:
1. When can you claim universal credit?
2. How do you transfer to universal credit?

What you need to know

- People already getting the 'legacy benefits' and tax credits that universal credit replaces are being moved to claims for universal credit in the 'managed migration' process.
- Many awards of legacy benefits have already been ended and replaced by universal credit. The managed migration process is due to be applied to people with remaining awards of legacy benefits during 2025.
- You can also transfer to universal credit before you are affected by the managed migration process if you decide to make a claim for universal credit yourself. This may be, for example, if your circumstances change and you need to make a new claim for benefit or if you believe you would be better off on universal credit. This is 'natural migration'.

1. When can you claim universal credit?

You can apply for universal credit at any time. However, if you currently get a 'means-tested benefit' there is an official scheme to transfer you to universal credit by ending your current award and inviting you to claim universal credit instead.

If you are still getting one of the 'legacy benefits' and tax credits that universal credit replaces, the DWP will notify you when you need to claim universal credit instead. This is the 'managed migration' transfer process. Before you are notified, you can transfer to universal credit if you make a claim for it yourself. You are not automatically entitled to universal credit.

If you move to universal credit under the managed migration process and are entitled to it, your award should not be worth less than your old award of legacy benefits and tax credits. This is called 'transitional protection' and it will reduce over time. But if you decide to claim universal credit before you come under the managed migration process, transitional protection does not apply – so you could be worse off straight away.

How does universal credit affect your other benefits and tax credits?

Universal credit replaces the means-tested benefits and tax credits for working-age people. You cannot make a new claim for any of these benefits, with the exception of housing benefit if you live in certain types of accommodation ('specified' or 'temporary' accommodation – see Box A).

> Box A
> **Specified and temporary accommodation**
>
> 'Specified accommodation' is accommodation where you can get certain types of help or support. It includes:
>
> - accommodation provided by housing associations, charities and some councils where care, support or supervision is provided
> - temporary accommodation for people who have left home because of domestic abuse – sometimes called 'emergency' temporary accommodation
>
> 'Temporary accommodation' is homeless accommodation where you do not get care, support or supervision, and for which you pay rent to a local authority or a provider of social housing.

You can get child benefit, disability benefits and other 'non-means-tested benefits', including contribution-based jobseeker's allowance and contributory employment and support allowance, at the same time as universal credit. These benefits are not being replaced by universal credit.

People under pension age can still make a claim for housing benefit if they live in certain types of specified and temporary accommodation.

> **EXAMPLE**
>
> **Help with rent in specified accommodation**
>
> Leo is getting income-related employment and support allowance and moves into specified rented accommodation. He can make a new claim for housing benefit (rather than universal credit) to help with the rent for the accommodation. As Leo has not yet claimed universal credit, his income-related employment and support allowance can continue for now.

Under the universal credit system, contribution-based jobseeker's allowance is referred to as 'new-style' jobseeker's allowance and contributory employment and support allowance as 'new-style' employment and support allowance. Both these benefits depend on your national insurance contribution record. If your income is low enough, they can be topped up with universal credit.

> Box B
> **Pension credit**
>
> Pension credit is not being replaced by universal credit, but you cannot get pension credit and universal credit at the same time.
>
> If you are in a couple and one of you is over pension age and the other under pension age, you can stay on pension credit if you already get it, but you cannot usually make a new claim for pension credit while one of you is under pension age, and you

must claim universal credit instead. There is more about this in Chapter 10.

If you can get pension credit, you may also still be able to get housing benefit.

If you (and your partner, if in a couple) were of pension age and getting child tax credit but not working tax credit, during 2024 you would have been invited to claim pension credit instead. If you (and your partner, if in a couple) were of pension age and getting working tax credit, during 2024 you would instead have been invited to claim universal credit under the managed migration process.

What CPAG says

Problems claiming new-style jobseeker's allowance and employment and support allowance

You may be told that contribution-based jobseeker's allowance and contributory employment and support allowance no longer exist or that you cannot claim them under the universal credit system. That is incorrect. Universal credit only replaces *income-based* jobseeker's allowance and *income-related* employment and support allowance.

Under the universal credit system, contribution-based jobseeker's allowance and contributory employment and support allowance are called 'new-style' jobseeker's allowance and 'new-style' employment and support allowance, and can be claimed alongside universal credit. However, a claim for either will terminate any entitlement you already have to income-based jobseeker's allowance or income-related employment and support allowance.

Do you have to claim universal credit?

No one is forced to make a claim for universal credit. In practice, however, sometimes you may feel that you have little choice. If you are making a new claim, you cannot do this for any means-tested benefits (except housing benefit if you live in specified accommodation or temporary accommodation), so you can only apply for universal credit. When you are affected by the managed migration transfer to universal credit, the DWP will stop your legacy benefits even if you do not claim universal credit – so if you do not claim, you will not have any means-tested benefit.

If you are already getting legacy benefits and tax credits, sometimes you may need to claim universal credit even before you are affected by the managed migration transfer process. For example, if you move to a new local authority area and your housing benefit ends, you will probably need to claim universal credit to get help with the rent.

You may believe that you would be better off on universal credit and you can make a claim for universal credit before you come under the managed migration process.

But if you claim universal credit before you come under that process, even if you are entitled to universal credit there is no guarantee that your initial award will be worth as much as your legacy benefits were.

2. How do you transfer to universal credit?

You transfer to universal credit from 'legacy benefits' when you make a claim for it. The DWP calls this 'migration' to universal credit.

There are two ways of migrating to universal credit.

- **'Managed migration'**: under this official process, the DWP tells you that your legacy benefit or tax credit will end and that you will need to claim universal credit instead. You do not have a choice about your old benefit or tax credit ending. Most people getting tax credits have already been migrated under this process. People getting income-related employment and support allowance but not child tax credit will be migrated by the end of 2025.

- **'Natural migration'**: this happens when you are already getting one of the legacy benefits or tax credits and you decide to claim universal credit, before you come under the managed migration process. This could be, for example, because your circumstances have changed and you need to make a new claim to get more help straight away, but as you cannot make a new claim for one of the legacy benefits, you claim universal credit. Also, you may believe that you would be better off on universal credit, so decide to make a claim in order to transfer to universal credit. You can make a claim for universal credit at any time.

What CPAG says

Migration to universal credit

It is only under the managed migration process that you are covered by rules providing 'transitional protection', intended to ensure that your initial award of universal credit is not worth less than your old award of legacy benefit.

If you are considering transferring to universal credit by natural migration, get advice about what that might mean for you. Remember that entitlement to universal credit is not guaranteed, and you cannot go back to the old means-tested benefit and tax credit system.

If you believe you would be better off on universal credit, try to check that in advance by using online benefit calculators and getting advice. Online benefit calculators are available at gov.uk/benefits-calculators. There is no guarantee that you will indeed be better off or in fact not be worse off if you migrate to universal credit via natural migration. If you would be worse off, you should wait until the DWP tells you that you need to claim universal credit.

Managed migration

The DWP may contact you to say that your legacy benefits are due to end from a certain date, and 'invite' you to claim universal credit instead. When you claim as part of this official process, this is called 'managed migration' to universal credit.

Managed migration applies if you are under pension age, or if you are in a couple and one of you is under pension age. If you (and your partner if you are in a couple) are of pension age and were getting working tax credit, you will also have been included in this process during 2024.

When the process begins, the DWP writes to you, notifying you of when you will be affected. Until then, you cannot transfer to universal credit by this process.

Box C
The managed migration process

1. The DWP sends you a 'migration notice', informing you that your legacy benefits and tax credits awards will end (on your 'deadline day') and that you need to make a claim for universal credit instead. When you are sent the migration notice, you become a 'notified person'.

2. You are given a date by which you must make your universal credit claim (your deadline day). This must be at least three months from the date of your migration notice. You can be given longer to claim universal credit if the DWP agrees you have a good reason, such as if you are unwell or need to arrange for help to make your claim.

3. Your entitlement to the legacy benefits ends (with a two-week 'run-on', as long as you would have remained entitled) when you claim universal credit or, if you do not claim, on the day before your deadline day. As long as you claim universal credit within a month of your deadline day (ie, by your your 'final deadline'), you can still get universal credit under this process.

> 4. You must verify your identity and attend an interview after you have submitted your online claim form. If you do not do so, the DWP will refuse you universal credit.

The DWP planned to notify most people getting legacy benefits through the managed migration process during 2024. Those getting income-related employment and support allowance but not child tax credit were due to be included in the process by the end of 2025.

You are not automatically entitled to universal credit – you must still satisfy the usual rules of entitlement. These are explained in Chapter 3. More information about making a claim is in Chapter 4.

What CPAG says

Managed migration

There is no choice about being affected by the managed migration process. Even if you do not claim universal credit, your legacy benefits will stop. It is unlikely that refusing to claim universal credit by the date you are given will be in your best interests.

If the DWP tells you that you will need to claim via the managed migration process, but you need more time to claim universal credit (eg, because you are unwell), contact the DWP and explain why you need more time. The DWP can cancel your migration notice if it considers this necessary to protect your interests. If you have complex needs and may be more vulnerable during the transfer process, the DWP should proceed with particular care and give you time to get assistance if necessary. However, there are no special rules about this.

If you would be worse off on universal credit, your benefit should include a transitional element, provided you claim universal credit within the time allowed and you are then entitled to universal credit. If you claim later, you have not transferred to universal credit under the managed migration process and are not entitled to any of this transitional protection.

Some people are better off on universal credit. If you would be worse off after transferring via managed migration, you are entitled to transitional protection. This is a top-up amount of universal credit (called a 'transitional element') so you do not lose out. For more on the transitional element and how it is calculated, see Chapter 5.

Natural migration

If you decide to claim for universal credit before you come under the managed migration process, this is called 'natural migration' to universal credit. Your entitlement to your legacy benefits and tax credits stops, and you cannot go back to them.

> **EXAMPLES**
>
> **Natural migration**
>
> Karim is getting income-related employment and support allowance, which includes the severe disability premium. When he moves into standard rented accommodation and needs help with the rent, he cannot make a new claim for housing benefit and must claim universal credit instead. Claiming universal credit ends Karim's entitlement to income-related employment and support allowance.
>
> Shereen gets income-related employment and support allowance and housing benefit. She moves to a different flat. Because this is in the same local authority area, she does not need to make a new housing benefit claim and both her housing benefit and income-related employment and support allowance continue. Shereen moves again, this time to a property in a different local authority area. Her current housing benefit claim comes to an end. Shereen is not in specified or temporary accommodation, and so cannot make a new claim for housing benefit. Instead, she claims universal credit. She has now transferred to universal credit via natural migration, and her entitlement to income-related employment and support allowance ends, whether or not she is actually entitled to universal credit.

Note: there is no guarantee that you will be entitled to universal credit, or that your initial award will be as much as your old award of legacy benefits. You cannot return to legacy benefits. So you should get advice before transferring to universal credit in this way. However, if you are severely disabled you may be entitled to a 'transitional SDP element', which is explained in the section 'Are you worse off on universal credit?' below.

Are you worse off on universal credit?

When you migrate to universal credit, the amount of benefit you get is likely to change. Some people are better off (this is more likely if they are working and have childcare costs), but some people are worse off. In particular, you may be worse off on universal credit if you have a disability or if you have a disabled child. This is because (unlike the legacy benefits) universal credit does not always include extra amounts specifically for disabled adults, and the amount for a disabled child is lower.

If you transfer to universal credit via managed migration, you are supposed to be protected from being worse off by transitional protection. If you would be worse off, your universal credit includes a transitional element to ensure that at the point of transfer your universal credit is not lower than your old legacy benefit and tax credit award. The transitional element reduces (or 'erodes') over time, as your universal credit amounts increase. Chapter 5 explains this in more detail.

If, instead, you transfer to universal credit via natural migration, your initial award of universal credit does not include any transitional protection. So it is always best to get advice about whether you will be better or worse off on universal credit before claiming. Independent online benefit calculators are available at gov.uk/benefits-calculators.

If you were entitled to a 'severe disability premium' in your old benefit and you transferred to universal credit by natural migration, you may be entitled to an extra amount of universal credit. You can also be entitled to this extra amount if you transfer under the managed migration process, but only if you do not get a transitional element, so in practice this is very unlikely. A severe disability premium was included in your (or your partner's) means-tested benefit if you (or your partner) were getting a qualifying disability benefit (such as the 'daily living component' of personal independence payment), no one got carer's allowance for looking after you, and you technically counted as living alone.

The DWP calls this extra amount of universal credit a 'transitional SDP element'. Until February 2024, this element was only supposed to compensate you for no longer having a severe disability premium. From February 2024, if that applies and you were also entitled to other disability premiums in your legacy benefit (or the lower amount of the disabled child element in child tax credit), then the amount of the transitional SDP element is increased so as also to compensate you for no longer having those premiums. The transitional SDP element reduces (erodes) over time in the same way as the transitional element does.

> **EXAMPLE**
>
> **Transitional SDP element**
>
> Salwa had been getting income-related employment and support allowance with a severe disability premium included. She had not yet been subject to managed migration to universal credit. She made a joint claim for universal credit with her husband – ie, natural migration to universal credit. They were both entitled to and awarded universal credit, including a transitional SDP element for Salwa. A year later, Salwa and her husband separate. This is a change of circumstances that means Salwa is no longer entitled to the transitional SDP element.

What CPAG says

No one worse off on universal credit?

At one time, the government claimed that no one would be worse off on universal credit. However, the only people fully protected from being worse off are those who transfer to universal credit under the official managed migration process, and even this protection is not intended to be permanent.

The protection from being worse off under the managed migration process is in the form of the transitional element of universal credit. But this transitional protection is only intended to ensure that the universal credit is not worth less than the old legacy benefit and tax credit at the point when you transfer to universal credit. Over time, the transitional element reduces (or 'erodes') as other universal credit amounts are increased. So, transitional protection is not forever and can be lost quite quickly.

There is no such transitional protection for people who instead transfer to universal credit under natural migration. However, if you are entitled to a severe disability premium in your legacy benefit, your universal credit should include a transitional SDP element to compensate you for your universal credit not including that premium and (since February 2024) other disability premiums. This is not a guarantee of not being worse off overall as soon as you claim and, like the transitional element, the transitional SDP element will reduce (or erode) over time. So it is vital to get advice before starting natural migration and claiming universal credit. It may be better, if you can, to wait until you come under the managed migration process.

Chapter 3
Who can get universal credit

This chapter covers:

1. Who can get universal credit?
2. What are the basic rules?
3. What are the financial conditions?
4. Can you get any other financial help?

What you need to know

- To get universal credit, you must meet the basic rules of entitlement and the financial conditions.
- The basic rules are about your age, residence in Great Britain, whether you are in education and accepting a 'claimant commitment'. The claimant commitment is an agreement of what you must do in return for receiving universal credit.
- The financial conditions are about your income and capital (such as savings, investments and certain types of property). You cannot get universal credit if your capital is above £16,000 (although some capital is ignored).
- Usually, if you are in a couple, both of you must meet the basic rules and the financial conditions.

1. Who can get universal credit?

Universal credit is a 'means-tested benefit' for both single people and couples on a low income to provide financial support for living costs, children, disability, housing costs and other needs. You can get universal credit whether you are in or out of work.

You can get universal credit if you meet the basic rules of entitlement and the financial conditions. As long as you meet those conditions, you can get universal credit regardless of your particular circumstances. For example, you can claim universal credit if you are:

- a parent, including a lone parent
- ill or disabled
- a carer
- unemployed
- employed or self-employed

EXAMPLES

Who can get universal credit

Ben has been made redundant. Depending on his income and his other circumstances, he can get universal credit to provide him with some financial help.

Sarah Ann is a lone parent working 12 hours a week in a low-paid job. She has two children and they live in a housing association flat. She can claim universal credit to provide her with some financial help.

Your specific circumstances are taken into account to decide how much universal credit you get and what you are expected to do to earn more or move towards work. There is more information in Chapter 5 on the amount of universal credit you can get, and in Chapter 6 on the 'work-related requirements' you may need to satisfy.

Couples

If you are in a couple, you will normally make a joint claim with your partner. Usually, both of you must satisfy the basic rules of entitlement and the financial conditions.

You count as a member of a couple if you are living together and are married or civil partners, or if you are living together and cohabiting. In some circumstances, you must claim as a single person, even though you are in a couple – eg, if your partner is under 18, but you are not. Chapter 4 contains some examples and more information about claiming universal credit.

In two circumstances, it is possible to get universal credit as a couple even though one of you does not meet the basic rules. These are: if one of you has reached pension age and the other has not, or if one of you is a student and the other is not.

> **EXAMPLE**
>
> **One member of a couple is a student**
>
> Irina is on a full-time undergraduate course and her partner is unemployed. They have no children. They can claim universal credit as a couple, even though Irina is a student.

If you are in a couple and *your partner* has not accepted a 'claimant commitment' outlining what you must do in order to receive universal credit, but *you* have, you cannot get universal credit. You must each accept your own claimant commitment to qualify. Chapter 6 has more information about the claimant commitment.

Who cannot get universal credit?

If you are in prison, you can get universal credit for your housing costs for up to six months, but only if you were getting housing costs in your universal credit award before going into prison. It must not be likely that you will be in prison for more than six months.

You cannot get universal credit if you are fully maintained by a religious order.

> **EXAMPLE**
>
> **Who cannot get universal credit**
>
> Vince is sentenced to 18 months in prison. He was getting universal credit that included an amount for his housing costs before he went into prison, but cannot continue to receive this because he is likely to be in prison for more than six months. If he were likely to be released within six months, he could get universal credit for his housing costs for up to six months of his time in prison.

2. What are the basic rules?

To be entitled to universal credit, you must meet certain basic rules. There are some exceptions, which are explained in this section.

You meet the basic rules for universal credit if:

- you are aged 18 or over
- you are under pension age
- you are not a student in education
- you are resident in Great Britain
- you accept a 'claimant commitment'

> **EXAMPLE**
>
> **The basic rules**
>
> Miriam and Chris are a British couple, both aged 20. They are not students. Can they claim universal credit?
>
> They meet the age rules, they are in Great Britain and they are not in education, so they can claim universal credit. They must claim jointly as a couple. They must each also accept a claimant commitment to meet certain 'work-related requirements'. If they satisfy all of these conditions, as well as the financial conditions, then they will be awarded universal credit.

Are you under 18?

The general rules are that you must be aged 18 or over to claim universal credit. However, there are exceptions. You can claim universal credit when you are aged 16 or 17 if:

- you are responsible for a child
- your partner has a child or 'qualifying young person' for whom they are responsible
- you are pregnant and your baby is due within 11 weeks, or you have given birth within the last 15 weeks
- you have 'limited capability for work' or you are waiting for an assessment
- you are a carer and have 'regular and substantial caring responsibilities'
- you are 'without parental support' (see Box A)

> **Box A**
> **Without parental support**
>
> You are without parental support if you have no parents, or you are living away from your parents (or someone acting in their place) because you are estranged from them or because there is a risk to your health if you lived with them, or your parents cannot support you because they are ill, disabled, in prison or not allowed to enter Great Britain. If you are looked after by the local authority, or someone else (such as a grandparent) is acting in place of a parent, you are not without parental support.

Note: if you claim universal credit for yourself, your parent cannot continue to claim benefit for you, so it may be important to check this before you claim.

If you are aged 16 or 17 and are in education, see page 24 for when you may be able to get universal credit while studying.

If you are a care leaver aged 16 or 17, you can only get universal credit if you or your partner have a child, or if you are ill or disabled (and have limited capability for work or you are waiting for an assessment). Your universal credit does not include housing costs.

Are you over pension age?

To get universal credit as a single person, you must be below pension age. Pension age is currently 66 for both men and women and is gradually rising to 67 by 2028.

If you are getting universal credit and form a couple with someone over pension age, you must claim universal credit as a couple (you cannot get both universal credit and pension credit). There is more information about this in Chapter 10.

> **EXAMPLE**
>
> **One member of a couple is over pension age**
>
> Lydia is 58 and gets universal credit. She moves in with her partner Josh, who is 66 and gets an occupational pension. They claim universal credit as a couple.
>
> Lydia must meet work-related requirements as a condition of getting universal credit, but Josh does not need to as he is over pension age.

Are you a student?

In general, you cannot get universal credit if you are a student. This is called 'receiving education' by the DWP. However, there are some exceptions.

> Box B
> **Who is a student?**
>
> - You are a student while you are on a full-time course of advanced education. This is a course above A level (or equivalents like Scottish highers and NVQ level 3) that leads to a higher education qualification such as an undergraduate or postgraduate degree, or diplomas of higher education or at Higher National Certificate level or above.

- From your 16th birthday to 1 September after your 19th birthday, you are a student if you are at, or accepted for, school or college on a non-advanced course (eg, below degree or Higher National Certificate level), or you are in training that is 'approved' by the DWP.
- You are a student while you are on another kind of full-time course, either advanced or non-advanced, if you can get a student loan or grant for your maintenance.
- Even if you are not in one of the above three groups, you count as a student if your course is not compatible with the hours that you are expected to be looking for work or with any other work-related requirements you are expected to meet for your universal credit claim.

Which students can get universal credit?
You can get universal credit while you are student if you are in one of the following groups.

- You have a child.
- You are a single foster parent (including some kinship carers).
- You are a foster parent and your partner is also a full-time student.
- You are disabled and get either disability living allowance, child disability payment, personal independence payment or adult disability payment and you were assessed as having limited capability for work before you started your course.
- You are aged under 22, without parental support, and on a non-advanced course which you started before your 21st birthday.
- You are a member of a couple and your partner is not a student, or your partner is a student but would be eligible for universal credit themself while studying.

- You have taken time out from your course due to illness or caring responsibilities, and you are waiting to rejoin your course, as you have recovered or your caring responsibilities have ended.
- You are over pension age.

How much universal credit you get, if any, depends on your income. Student loans and some maintenance grants count as income, but usually only during the academic year. Chapter 5 explains how your universal credit is calculated.

What CPAG says

Problems with student claims

If you are a student and are in one of the above groups, but you are told you cannot get universal credit, ask for a 'mandatory reconsideration' of this decision. As long as you meet one of the above conditions, you are eligible for universal credit, even though you are a student. The DWP sometimes makes errors and assumes you cannot get universal credit if you are studying.

EXAMPLES

Students who can get universal credit

William is on a full-time advanced course. He claims universal credit. He is disabled and gets personal independence payment. He gets contributory employment and support allowance and has been assessed as having limited capability for work before he started his course. He is entitled to universal credit.

Camila is on a full-time advanced course and is a lone parent. She can claim universal credit.

Residence in Great Britain

In general, you must be resident in Great Britain to claim universal credit, although there are exceptions to this. You may also have to be 'habitually resident' before you can get universal credit. In broad terms, this means that you have been living here for a while and intend to stay for some time to come.

Are you going abroad?

You can continue to get universal credit while abroad for up to one month. You must usually continue to meet your work-related requirements. There are only limited circumstances when you can get universal credit for longer than this – eg, for up to two months if a close relative has died or for up to six months if the trip is to get medical treatment. If you stay at home and your partner is abroad for longer than a month, the amount of your universal credit usually decreases, so it is important to tell the DWP. Some people who work abroad can get universal credit – eg, members of the armed forces.

Have you come to Great Britain from abroad?

In some cases, if you have come from abroad you cannot get universal credit, even though you are resident in Great Britain.

You must have a 'right to reside' in Great Britain to get universal credit. If you are a British citizen, you have a right to reside.

Following the UK leaving the European Union (EU), the current rules mean that only certain people can continue to rely on European rights to establish a right to reside to access benefits.

Unless you are a British or Irish citizen or are someone who can continue to rely on European rights, then from 1 January 2021, you must have leave to enter or remain under UK immigration law that provides a right to reside. Under the EU Settlement Scheme, only 'settled' status counts to give access to universal credit. 'Pre-settled' status alone is not sufficient for access to universal credit.

You cannot usually get universal credit if you are defined as a 'person subject to immigration control'. You will usually have 'no recourse to public funds' stamped in your passport or stated in the document issued to you confirming your leave to remain. This means you cannot claim most social security benefits, including universal credit.

People who have refugee leave, humanitarian protection or discretionary leave, and those in some other circumstances, can get universal credit.

> **EXAMPLES**
>
> **Right to reside**
>
> Renee is French and arrived in the UK in November 2018. She has been working full time in Great Britain since January 2019. She applied for leave under the EU Settlement Scheme and has been granted pre-settled status. She can continue to rely on her European rights to establish a right to reside as a worker and access universal credit.
>
> Karolina is Lithuanian and plans to come to the UK in July 2025. As Karolina is not a British or Irish citizen and is not someone who can continue to rely on her European rights to establish a right to reside, she will need to have leave to enter and remain in the UK under immigration law. Unless her leave specifies that she has access to benefits, she cannot get universal credit.

The residence rules can be very complicated, so seek advice if you are affected by them.

Accepting a claimant commitment

To be entitled to universal credit, you must usually accept a claimant commitment. The claimant commitment sets out what you must do to receive your universal credit award. The key part of a claimant commitment is about your work-related requirements. There is more information about the claimant commitment in Chapter 6.

3. What are the financial conditions?

To be entitled to universal credit, your income must be sufficiently low. How much income you can have and still be entitled to some universal credit depends on your circumstances. Usually, as your income increases, the amount of universal credit you get decreases. If you have a partner, it is your combined income that counts.

Your capital (eg, savings and investments) must not be more than £16,000. If it is higher than £16,000, you are not entitled to universal credit. If you have a partner, it is your combined capital that counts. **Note:** capital over £16,000 is disregarded for 12 assessment periods if you are transferred to universal credit from tax credits under the 'managed migration' process.

There is more information about the income and capital rules in Chapter 5.

You must also meet the basic rules.

4. Can you get any other financial help?

If you get universal credit, you may be eligible for the following.

- A Sure Start maternity grant. This is a grant (£500 in 2024/25) to help with the costs of a newborn baby, usually only if there is no other child younger than 16 in your family. In Scotland, you are eligible for a Best Start grant instead.

- Healthy Start vouchers (for milk, fruit and vegetables) and vitamins if you are pregnant or have a young child. In Scotland, you may be eligible for a Best Start foods payment instead.

- Help with council tax if you are on a low income. Apply to your local council tax reduction scheme.

- A funeral expenses payment to cover basic funeral costs. In Scotland, you are eligible for funeral support payment instead.

- In England and Wales, a cold weather payment for weeks when the temperature is below freezing. In Scotland, a winter heating payment (if you get universal credit) during the first week in November.

- Free prescriptions, NHS sight tests, vouchers for glasses, dental treatment and fares to hospital. You are only eligible if your monthly earnings are no more than £435, or £935 if you have the 'child element' or 'limited capability for work' or 'limited capability for work-related activity' element included in your universal credit award. **Note:** prescriptions are free for everyone in Wales and Scotland, and NHS sight tests are free for everyone in Scotland.

Universal credit may also help you qualify for other help. This is known as 'passporting'. You may also have to have earnings below a certain amount to qualify.

Other financial help includes:

- free school lunches (in primary school for at least the first three years and on the basis of passporting thereafter)
- school clothing grants
- help with heating and energy efficiency measures
- legal aid
- local leisure facility discounts
- social tariffs from utility companies

Some schemes are administered by central government departments, some by the Scottish and Welsh governments, and some by local authorities or other agencies. Some of this passported help is provided in cash or vouchers, and some as discounts on charges.

In general, you must make a separate claim for the passported help.

Further information

There is more information about who can get universal credit and the other benefits you may qualify for in CPAG's *Welfare Benefits Handbook*.

There is more information about when a person can rely on European rights to access benefits in CPAG's *Benefits for Migrants Handbook*.

Chapter 4
Claiming universal credit

This chapter covers:

1. Who should claim universal credit?
2. How do you make a claim?
3. When should you claim?
4. How are you paid?
5. What happens if your circumstances change?

What you need to know

- Couples make a joint claim for universal credit. If you are a lone parent or a single person, you make a single claim. The usual way to claim is online, although phone claims can be made in certain circumstances.

- Universal credit is normally paid directly into your bank account. Couples may have a joint account or can choose which partner should be paid.

- Payments are usually made monthly. There are alternative arrangements if you are in exceptional circumstances and need help managing your money. If you live in Scotland, you can ask to be paid fortnightly.

- Unless you are told otherwise, you do not need to report changes in your earnings, but you must report any other changes in your circumstances.

1. Who should claim universal credit?

You claim for yourself if you are single or a lone parent. If you are in a couple, you make a joint claim with your partner. However, if you are in a couple and one of you does not meet the basic rules for universal credit (eg, if they are abroad or away from home for an extended period, or if they are under 18), you cannot make a joint claim: you must claim as a single person. It is important to give details about both of you when you claim, because even though you do not get an amount for your partner in your award, you are usually still treated as a couple for other parts of the assessment. So, for example, your joint income and capital are taken into account, and your partner's circumstances count when deciding whether you can get any help with childcare costs.

> **EXAMPLES**
>
> **Claiming universal credit**
>
> Lauren is 17 and lives with her partner Cameron, who is 18 and looking for work. Cameron claims universal credit as a single person because Lauren is not entitled as a 17 year old. His standard allowance is the amount for a single person.
>
> Kyle is 19. He lives with his 17-year-old partner Deepti and their baby. Because Deepti has a child and so is entitled to universal credit as a 17 year old, they can make a joint claim.

If you have been claiming universal credit jointly as a couple but have now separated from your partner, tell the DWP. You can both stay on universal credit as single people without having to make new claims.

If you become a couple (ie, you and your partner start living together), you do not need to make a new claim if one or both of you is already getting universal credit. Tell the DWP about the change in your situation and provide any information required. If one partner was getting 'means-tested benefits' or tax credits, tell the DWP or Tax Credit Office. You cannot get the old means-tested benefits and tax credits at the same time as universal credit, so these will stop. There is more about this in Chapter 2.

2. How do you make a claim?

You claim universal credit online at gov.uk/universal-credit/how-to-claim. There is no paper claim form. If you need help with this, call the free universal credit helpline for help from the DWP (Monday to Friday 8am to 6pm: 0800 328 5644; textphone 0800 328 1344; Welsh language 0800 328 1744. This service includes a video relay service for British Sign Language (BSL) users). Alternatively you can contact the free Help to Claim phone service run by Citizens Advice (details at citizensadvice.org.uk/helptoclaim. This service includes help via Relay UK if you cannot speak or hear on the phone, or via the video relay service for BSL users).

> Box A
> **Completing the online claim form**
> - When you are ready to claim, make sure you have the following information to hand:
>   - your email address
>   - your mobile phone number
>   - details of the people who live with you, such as your partner, children or lodgers
>   - details of your housing circumstances and costs
>   - details of any income, such as payslips or other benefits
>   - any savings or capital, such as shares or property that you rent to others
>   - details of any health conditions you have
>   - details of any education or training you are undertaking
>   - details and registration number of your childcare provider
>   - details of the bank account you want your universal credit paid into – either your own account or a joint account with your partner
>   - verification of your identity, such as a debit or credit card, a recent bank statement, driving licence or passport
> - Completing the claim is likely to take up some time – often about 40 minutes.

- First, you are asked to set up an online account by entering a username, password and answering two security questions. You must also give your email address.
- If you do not have all the information you need to make the claim, you can log in again at any time during the next 28 days to complete the form, but your date of claim will only be from the date you submit your completed form. As such, if it may be better to submit the claim straight away if you are able (letting the DWP know you are doing this) and then provide the missing information at the earliest possible stage.
- You are asked to verify your identity online. If you cannot manage this, your identity can be verified at the job centre instead. You should be given at least a month to arrange and attend the interview at the job centre.
- If you are claiming as a couple, both you and your partner must make an online claim. The first person is given a 'linking code' to give to their partner, so that the two claims can be linked together as one.
- When you get to the end of your online claim, you are given a summary of the information you have entered. You have a chance to go back and correct any mistakes. When you are happy that the information is correct, submit your claim.

After you submit your claim, you are given a phone number to book an appointment for an interview at your local job centre. Couples must both attend.

At the interview, you are asked to confirm your identity and sign a copy of your claim details. You will meet your 'work coach' and agree what you will do next to look for or prepare for work. This goes into your 'claimant commitment', which is a record of what you are expected to do. You must sign this, otherwise your claim will be refused.

What CPAG says

Making a successful claim

It can be difficult to get through all the stages of the universal credit claims process. As well as submitting an online claim, you must verify your identity, either online or in person at the job centre, and first book and then attend an interview to agree a claimant commitment. Some claimants, particularly those not from the UK, may also need to attend a 'habitual residence test' appointment to prove their eligibility. If you miss any of these stages, your claim will be 'closed' and you are not paid.

- Ask for help if you have any difficulty with your claim. Call the DWP on the free universal credit helpline or contact your local job centre. You can find the address and phone number of your local job centre at gov.uk/contact-jobcentre-plus. Alternatively, contact the free Help to Claim service run by Citizens Advice (citizensadvice.org.uk/helptoclaim).

- If you are helping someone to claim, remember that many people also need help to book and attend their interview. Some people who manage to submit an online claim find their claim is closed (ie, they are refused universal credit) because they do not book or attend the interview.

- If your claim is refused because you missed an interview or appointment, make a new claim as soon as you can. Ask for the new claim to be backdated if any difficulty you had was connected to a disability or ill health. Ask for compensation if the DWP gave you the wrong advice or made it hard for you to get through the process.

- If the DWP closes your claim, it has made a decision that you are not entitled to universal credit. You can appeal against this. First ask for a 'mandatory reconsideration' of the decision. You can do this online if you have made a new claim, but otherwise you will need to do this by phone or post as you will no longer be able to write on your journal.

You receive a text or email in your online journal when the decision on your universal credit claim is available. The decision is described as your universal credit 'statement' and you get one of these each month. This gives details of how the amount of your award has been worked out, including which 'elements' are included and any deductions for earnings and other income. The decision tells you about your appeal rights.

Are you unable to claim online?

If you do not have online access at home or you are unable to use the internet, your local job centre may be able to help you or direct you to local organisations that can help you make your claim. The free Help to Claim phone service run by Citizens Advice can provide help in making your claim and getting your first payment.

If you cannot claim online, you may be allowed to claim by telephone in certain circumstances, such as if you have a visual impairment, lack literacy skills or have physical or mental health conditions that would make managing an online claim difficult. A DWP employee takes your details and completes an online claim for you. If you cannot use the telephone, you can ask to claim in person – eg, at a local office or by the DWP visiting you at home. However, this is intended to be only for people with exceptional circumstances so may not be agreed. If you claim by phone or in person, your claim starts when you first contact the DWP to say you want to claim, so it is important to do so quickly if you cannot claim online.

If you cannot make a claim or act on your own behalf, perhaps because you have a mental health problem or learning disability, someone else (called an 'appointee') can be authorised to act on your behalf. This could be a friend or relative. The appointee not only makes the claim but also takes on your responsibilities as a claimant, such as reporting any changes in your circumstances.

Have you claimed universal credit before?

If you were getting universal credit in the past and your previous claim ended within the last six months, you can log into your previous online account to reclaim. Your new claim takes less time than your earlier one. You are paid on the same dates as before.

If you are reclaiming universal credit because your job has ended, try to restart your claim within seven days of the job ending, to ensure your first payment is backdated as far as possible. If you cannot do so and you have a good reason for the delay, your first payment will still be for the maximum amount.

If you have claimed universal credit before and, because your income was too high, that claim was refused or your award of universal credit was stopped, you can be automatically treated as claiming again during the following five monthly assessment periods that would have applied had you been awarded universal credit. If that applies to you, you are treated as claiming again during each of those five monthly periods, without you actually making a claim. This may help you if, having been refused universal credit or had your award stopped because your income was too high, your income decreases at some point in the following five months and the DWP is aware of that decrease.

3. When should you claim?

Usually, your entitlement to universal credit starts when you submit your claim, so it is important not to delay – claim as soon as you think you may be entitled. However, it is sometimes possible for a claim to be 'backdated'.

When can your claim be backdated?

Your claim can only be backdated in certain circumstances and for a maximum of one month. If any of the following apply to you and mean that you could not have reasonably claimed earlier, ask the DWP to backdate your claim for up to a month.

- You have a disability.
- You send a medical certificate to say that you could not claim earlier because you were ill.

- You were getting jobseeker's allowance or employment and support allowance which ended, but you were only notified after it ended.
- You could not claim online because the system was not working.
- You were in a couple, but are now claiming as a single person and your former partner did not accept a 'claimant commitment', which meant that your joint claim was refused or stopped.

If you are a couple claiming universal credit jointly, both of you must be in one of these circumstances.

> **EXAMPLES**
>
> **Backdating a claim**
>
> Demi is 20 and has just had her first baby. She is a lone parent. A week after the baby is born, she completes the online claim for universal credit. Her award is not backdated and she misses out on a week's money.
>
> Freddie has been in hospital after having a heart attack. He is self-employed and has not been able to work for three weeks. When he gets home, he claims universal credit. He asks for it to be backdated and sends in his medical certificate. The DWP accepts that it was not reasonable for him to have claimed earlier and backdates his award.
>
> Trevor lost his job after a deterioration in his mental health. As a result of his illness he did not claim universal credit for six weeks. After being in receipt of universal credit for two months, he learns that he might be entitled to a backdate. He requests this using his online journal, explaining his claim was delayed due to his mental ill health. Even though he has made this request after the claim has been decided, the DWP should consider revising his initial claim as if it was made up to a month earlier. This may mean Trevor is entitled to some additional money.

> **What CPAG says**
>
> **Backdating**
>
> The DWP previously had a policy of only allowing backdating of a claim when it was requested before the initial decision on entitlement to universal credit was made. However, it was found that this approach was not correct in law, as the rules do not specifically say backdating must be requested before the initial decision. You should still request backdating within a month of making your claim where possible, but if you could not do this before the initial decision on your claim was made, request backdating anyway and seek advice if your request is refused.

4. How are you paid?

Universal credit is usually paid directly into your bank or building society account in monthly payments. It is paid in arrears.

You must wait for one month and up to another seven days from the date you claim before you get your first payment. You are then paid on the same date each month. If this falls at a weekend or on a bank holiday, you are paid on the last working day before that. The amount you get does not change with the number of days in the month.

Each payment is based on your circumstances in the last monthly 'assessment period'. This is one calendar month, beginning with the first day of your entitlement to universal credit, and is the same date in each month after that.

If you are in a couple and claiming jointly, all your universal credit is usually paid to one of you. It is up to you to decide whose account it is paid into, or you can have a joint account. If you cannot decide, the DWP can make the decision.

If your partner will not let you have any of the money, you can ask the DWP to split the monthly payments between you, or pay them to you. The DWP must decide that it is in your, or your child's, interest to be paid in this way. These 'alternative payment arrangements' are meant to be exceptional to avoid hardship – eg, if there is domestic abuse or if your partner is not managing the household finances properly.

> **EXAMPLE**
>
> **When you are paid**
>
> Jamal is unemployed. He claims universal credit on 11 October. His first monthly assessment period starts on 11 October and ends on 10 November. He gets his first monthly payment of universal credit paid into his bank account seven days later on 17 November and on the 17th of each month after that.

Can you manage until your first payment?

It will be at least five weeks from submitting your claim before you are paid. Sometimes, the wait is much longer. At your initial interview at the job centre, you are asked whether you can manage until your first universal credit payment, and you may be offered a 'universal credit advance' to help tide you over. The advance is up to a full month's payment. You pay it back out of your universal credit award, which can mean large reductions in your payments for up to 24 months.

If, after your initial interview, you decide that you need an advance, you can apply through your online account or by phoning the universal credit helpline. You should apply before the end of the first 'assessment period'.

You can also ask for an advance while you wait for the amount of your universal credit award to increase after your circumstances change – eg, after you leave a job.

The DWP only gives you an advance if it considers you are in financial need – eg, if you cannot afford to pay your gas or electricity bills and are not owed any wages.

You cannot appeal if the DWP refuses to give you an advance or about the amount of your repayments. If you are refused an advance, provide more information about your situation and ask the DWP to reconsider its decision.

> **EXAMPLE**
>
> **Universal credit advance**
>
> Amber is a lone parent with one child. She works part time and rents her home. Amber claims universal credit. Her part-time wages are not enough to buy food and pay the bills. At her job centre interview, she asks for a universal credit advance to help her manage until her first payment. Her request is accepted and an advance of £1,200 is paid into her bank account five days later, estimated to be her full monthly award. Five weeks later, she receives her first monthly universal credit payment. She gets £1,150 a month because £50 is taken off each month to repay the advance.

You may be able to get help in a crisis from your local authority's local welfare assistance scheme.

Are monthly payments causing problems?

When you claim universal credit, you are offered advice about budgeting. This may be online, by telephone or in person at a local money advice service.

If the way you are paid is causing you difficulty, you can ask to be paid in a different way. Phone 0800 328 5644 or ask your 'work coach' at the job centre about alternative payment arrangements.

If you are accepted as eligible, there are three main alternative payment arrangements.

- You can be paid twice a month or, very exceptionally, four times a month.
- Your rent can be paid directly to your landlord.

- Your payment can be split between you and your partner.

The DWP decides whether you can be paid in one of the alternative ways. You cannot appeal if you disagree, but you can give more information about your situation and ask the DWP to reconsider. The decision is based on guidance and depends on your circumstances. The DWP reviews the arrangements after a period of time, usually from three months to two years.

If you live in Scotland and do not already have alternative payment arrangements in place, you can choose to be paid twice a month, and choose to have your rent paid directly to your landlord (called 'Scottish choices'). You do not have to show that you have difficulty managing monthly payments.

> Box B
> **Alternative payment arrangements**
>
> You are most likely to be accepted for an alternative payment arrangement if:
>
> - you have rent arrears or are threatened with eviction or repossession
> - you have severe debt problems
> - you have difficulty reading or writing, or with simple maths
> - you have a learning disability or a mental health condition
> - you have an alcohol, drug or gambling addiction
> - you are under 18 or a care leaver
> - you are homeless, or in temporary or supported accommodation
> - you are (or were) experiencing domestic abuse
> - you are a family with multiple or complex needs
>
> There are other reasons given in the government's guidance why someone might have difficulty managing, so it is worth explaining why you need this help.

What CPAG says

Avoiding rent arrears

You may find that you have built up rent arrears – either as a result of having to wait for your first payment of universal credit, or because the 'housing costs element' for your rent is not paid directly to your landlord. The following may help you avoid rent arrears.

- When you make your claim, make sure you report all the details of your rent. Remember that you are still liable to pay your rent. If you did not report your housing costs at first, ask that your universal credit be revised to have the correct amount included from the start of your claim.

- If you were previously getting housing benefit, you should get paid an extra two weeks 'run-on' of housing benefit when you make your universal credit claim to help tide you over until your first universal credit payment.

- Ask for a 'universal credit advance' if you need help while waiting for your first payment.

- You may be able to ask for alternative payment arrangements, so that you have your rent paid directly to your landlord. If you live in Scotland, you can choose to have your rent paid directly to your landlord, irrespective of your circumstances. Be aware that this may mean that your rent is paid on a different date to when it is due, so it can appear that you are in arrears – talk to your landlord if this happens.

Do you need a loan?

If you need a loan (eg, for a household item you cannot afford or to meet expenses for a new baby or a new job), you can ask for a 'budgeting advance' of universal credit. This is an interest-free loan of universal credit, which you must repay.

You can ask for a budgeting advance for whatever you need, but if you are refused you cannot appeal. To qualify, you must have been on universal credit (or income support, income-based jobseeker's allowance, income-related employment and support allowance or pension credit) for at least six months, unless you need the advance to help you get work or stay in work. Your earnings and any savings or capital resources must also be below a certain level. The maximum you can get depends on your family size. If you have a child, the current maximum (in 2024/25) is £812.

You repay the advance from your universal credit award each month – usually over a 12-month period, although that can be extended. The repayment period is due to be increased to two years for budgeting loans taken out from December 2024. You must pay it back in full before you can get another budgeting advance.

> **EXAMPLE**
>
> **Budgeting advance**
>
> Meira is a lone parent and is getting universal credit. Her washing machine has broken down and she needs a new one. Instead of buying one with expensive high street credit, she asks for a budgeting advance of her universal credit. She pays this back out of her monthly award over the next 12 months.

Can universal credit be paid to other people?

In some circumstances, the DWP can pay part of your universal credit to someone else on your behalf. For example, if you owe money for your fuel or water, the DWP can make deductions from your universal credit award and pay the money directly to the fuel or water company.

If you rent your home, normally the amount for rent in your universal credit is paid to you as part of your monthly award, not to your landlord. It is paid in this way irrespective of whether you rent from a local authority, housing association or private landlord. However, if you are finding it difficult to budget or are building up rent arrears, the DWP may decide to pay your landlord directly under the alternative payment arrangements. This can happen if either you or your landlord request direct payments. If you live in Scotland, you can ask that your rent be paid directly to your landlord – you do not need to have built up arrears.

Your landlord may also request that a deduction be made from your universal credit to pay towards rent arrears you have already accrued. They can only do this when you have two months' worth of rent arrears but do not require your permission.

5. What happens if your circumstances change?

Your circumstances may change while you are getting universal credit. The DWP tells you which changes you should report. You must report all these changes, as well as any other changes that might affect your universal credit award. It is best to report the change on your online journal, under the 'Report a change' section. If you do not have an online account or are struggling to access it, you can instead phone the universal credit helpline (Monday to Friday 8am to 6pm: 0800 328 5644; textphone 0800 328 1344; Welsh language 0800 328 1744; this service includes a video relay service for British Sign Language users) to report changes. You should report the change promptly and always before the end of the monthly 'assessment period' in which the change occurred.

If you are employed, you do not usually need to report changes in your earnings – the DWP gets this information from HM Revenue and Customs (HMRC) through its 'real-time information' system. Under this, your employer sends HMRC information about your earnings every time you are paid. However, you may be asked to report your earnings if, for example, your employer is not doing so properly or a report is missing or wrong. If you think the real-time information on your earnings is wrong, send information about what you think is the correct amount to the DWP, even if you have not been asked to report your earnings.

If you are self-employed, you are expected to report your earnings every month on a 'cash in/cash out' basis – ie, the income you have received during the month and payments you have made for that month for any permitted expenses.

If you pay for childcare, you may be asked to report your childcare charges each month.

> **EXAMPLE**
>
> **Reporting self-employed earnings**
>
> Damian is self-employed. He gets a message from the DWP reminding him to report his earnings for 12 February to 11 March (his monthly assessment period). Damian is busy and does not get round to it. His universal credit award is not paid when it is next due and the DWP tells him that it has been suspended. He must send in the missing earnings report quickly, otherwise his award will stop altogether.

How is your universal credit affected?

You are paid universal credit a month in arrears, so every payment you get is based on your circumstances in the previous month. When you report a change in your circumstances, you must wait until your next universal credit payday before the amount of your award goes up or down. The revised amount is normally worked out as though your new circumstances had lasted for the whole of the previous month. A 'month' means the monthly assessment period on which your payment is based.

If you are late reporting a change (ie, you report it after the end of the assessment period in which the change took place) and the amount of your universal credit increases because of the change, you are not paid arrears before the month you actually reported it, so you will lose money. The DWP can backdate the increase if there are special circumstances, so it is always worth saying why you are reporting a change late and explaining any difficulties you had, such as ill health.

> **EXAMPLES**
>
> **Changes in circumstances**
>
> Zanab has a new baby on 20 June. This is two weeks into her universal credit assessment period, which ends on 5 July. She tells the DWP on 1 July. Her next payment on 12 July includes an extra £287.92. This is the child element for the whole month in which her baby was born.
>
> Emma has a new baby on 10 July. This is one week into her universal credit assessment period, which ends on 2 August. She is depressed and tired and does not call the DWP until 5 August. She is paid her usual amount on 9 August, with no extra amount for her baby. She is paid an extra £287.92 for the baby on 9 September. She has lost a month's extra money. If Emma had explained why she was late reporting the birth, the DWP could have decided to pay the additional amount from 9 August.
>
> Ollie starts university on 6 October. This is three weeks into his universal credit assessment period, which ends on 14 October. He tells the DWP on 6 October. He is no longer entitled to universal credit as a student (none of the situations in which you can get it as a student apply to Ollie) and so his award stops. On his next payday on 21 October, he gets no universal credit.

If the amount of your universal credit decreases because of the change, this is backdated to the first day of the monthly assessment period in which the change occurred. So, if you are late reporting the change, you will have been overpaid. The later you report the change, the more the overpayment will be. There is more about overpayments in Chapter 8.

Further information

The DWP has produced a basic guide *Universal Credit and You*, available at gov.uk/government/publications/universal-credit-and-you. There is more detailed guidance available at gov.uk/government/collections/universal-credit-information-for-stakeholders-and-partners.

You can find details on your local authority's local welfare assistance scheme at advicelocal.uk.

More information about universal credit claims and payments is in CPAG's *Welfare Benefits Handbook*.

CPAG's *Mental Health and Benefits Handbook* has useful information about making a claim and providing evidence if you have a mental health problem.

Chapter 5
The amount of universal credit

This chapter covers:
1. What is the maximum amount of universal credit?
2. How do your income and capital affect universal credit?
3. How much universal credit do you get?

What you need to know

- Universal credit includes an amount for you and your partner. This is called the 'standard allowance'.

- A 'child element' is added to the standard allowance for a child or children for whom you are responsible. There is an additional amount if your child is disabled, called the 'disabled child addition'.

- Additional amounts known as 'elements' are added to the standard allowance, depending on your circumstances. You may get an additional element if you or your partner are ill or disabled, or if you or your partner are caring for a disabled person. There are also elements to help with your rent (and some 'service charges'), and for childcare costs.

- If you transfer to universal credit by 'managed migration', you may get an additional amount included (a 'transitional element') to ensure you are not financially worse off.

- If you have other income, this reduces the amount of universal credit to which you are entitled, although some income is ignored.

- You are not entitled to universal credit if you and your partner have more than £16,000 capital.

1. What is the maximum amount of universal credit?

Universal credit is a 'means-tested benefit'. This means that the amount you get depends on your family circumstances and on how much other income (if any) you have. As your income increases, the amount of your universal credit award decreases.

Your 'maximum universal credit' is made up of a 'standard allowance' and additional amounts (called 'elements') for:

- each child (limited to two children in some circumstances)
- each disabled child (at a lower or higher rate)
- you or your partner if you are ill or disabled
- you or your partner if you were previously entitled to the severe disability premium within certain 'legacy benefits' within the immediate one month before claiming universal credit and continue to meet the severe disability premium conditions during that month (there is more about this on page 74)
- you or your partner if you care for a disabled person
- your rent and certain service charges
- your childcare costs

If you transfer to universal credit by 'managed migration', you may also have a 'transitional element' included to ensure you are not worse off when you are transferred to universal credit from your legacy benefits.

Each of these amounts has its own qualifying conditions. The rest of this section explains when these elements are included in your universal credit and how your maximum amount of universal credit is worked out. If you have no income or your income is below a certain level, you get the maximum amount of universal credit. However, this may be reduced by the government's 'benefit cap'.

Standard allowance

Universal credit includes an amount for living costs for you and your partner, if you have one. This is called the standard allowance. How much you get depends on your age and whether you are claiming as a single person or jointly with your partner.

5 / The amount of universal credit

Monthly rates of standard allowance, 2024/25	
Single claimant, under 25	£311.68
Single claimant, 25 or over	£393.45
Joint claimants, both under 25	£489.23
Joint claimants, at least one 25 or over	£617.60

Child element

If you are responsible for any children, your universal credit includes an additional amount (called a 'child element') for each child under 16. You can also get a child element for each 'qualifying young person' who is aged 16 to 18 (or 19 in some cases) and who is, for example, still at school or college on a non-advanced course.

Note: you get a child element for all children born before 6 April 2017. You cannot usually get a child element for a third or subsequent child born on or after 6 April 2017, but there are exceptions. There is more information about the 'two-child limit' in Chapter 10.

Monthly rates of child element, 2024/25	
First child/qualifying young person if born before 6 April 2017	£333.33
Each other child/qualifying young person	£287.92

If your first or only child was born before 6 April 2017, the child element is £333.33. For any other child, regardless of their date of birth, the amount is £287.92. For example, if you have two children, both born after 6 April 2017, you get a child element of £287.92 for each child.

A child can only be included in one universal credit claim. So if your child normally lives with more than one person (eg, if you are separated from your partner and your child lives with both of you), whoever has the main responsibility for the child can claim universal credit for them.

You cannot normally be responsible for a child who is being 'looked after' by the local authority. The exceptions to this are if the child is living with you and you have parental responsibility for them, or if they are being looked after because they are away for a planned short respite break.

Disabled child addition

If your child is disabled, your universal credit includes an additional amount. There are two levels of payment, depending on the severity of your child's disability.

- You get the lower rate of the disabled child addition if your child gets disability living allowance, child disability payment, personal independence payment or adult disability payment.
- You get the higher rate of the disabled child addition if your child gets the highest rate 'care component' of disability living allowance or child disability payment or the enhanced rate of the 'daily living component' of personal independence payment or adult disability payment, or if they are certified as severely sight impaired or blind.
- Even if you do not get a child element for your child due to the two-child limit, you still get the disabled child addition if your child gets the appropriate qualifying benefits.

Monthly additional amounts for a disabled child, 2024/25	
Lower amount	£156.11
Higher amount	£487.58

Additional element if you or your partner are ill or disabled

If you or your partner are ill or disabled, you may be able to get an additional element added to your standard allowance. This is called the 'limited capability for work-related activity' element. You do not get this automatically. For example, you may get personal independence payment because of your disability, but this does not mean you get the limited capability for work-related activity element in your universal credit. To get the element, you must be assessed as having limited capability for work-related activity. Before 3 April 2017, a lower rate of the element was added to your standard allowance if you were assessed as having 'limited capability for work'. In general, if your period of limited capability for work started on or after 3 April 2017, the limited capability for work element is not included.

Monthly additional amounts for ill health or disability, 2024/25	
Limited capability for work element (only if your limited capability for work started before 3 April 2017)	£156.11
Limited capability for work-related activity element	£416.19

Note: although there is no additional amount for limited capability for work in new claims from 3 April 2017, it can still be important to be assessed as having limited capability for work. This is because you can keep a certain amount of your earnings before your universal credit is affected (called a 'work allowance') and you have fewer 'work-related requirements'.

In some circumstances, you are treated as having limited capability for work without having to be assessed. For example, this applies if you are a hospital patient (this can be extended from when you leave hospital until you have recovered), or if you are in residential rehabilitation for drug or alcohol problems.

In some circumstances, you can also be treated as having limited capability for work-related activity without having to be assessed. For example, this applies if you are terminally ill or you are having chemotherapy or radiotherapy for cancer (or are likely to do so in the next six months), or if you are recovering from this treatment. If you have already been assessed as having limited capability for work-related activity for employment and support allowance and are getting employment and support allowance on the date you claim universal credit, you are treated as having limited capability for work-related activity for universal credit and should get the element straight away.

> Box A
> **The work capability assessment**
>
> The 'work capability assessment' is an assessment that checks how your health conditions or disabilities affect your ability to work. The potential results of the work capability assessment are that you are 'fit for work', have limited capability for work or have limited capability for work-related activity. The assessment usually involves you completing a questionnaire and attending a medical examination. To pass the test, you must score 15 points on a list of specified activities, called 'descriptors'.
>
> If you are assessed as having limited capability for work-related activity, this generally means that your health conditions or disabilities are so serious that you should not be expected to think about returning to work at the moment.
>
> If you do not complete the questionnaire about your health problems or do not attend the medical without a good reason, you are likely to be treated as being fully capable to work.
>
> You may be regularly assessed to check whether you still meet the conditions.
>
> The work capability assessment is also used to decide whether you qualify for employment and support allowance. If you get employment and support allowance, you do not need to have a separate assessment for universal credit.

You do not get an additional element for limited capability for work-related activity in your universal credit straight away. There is usually a 'waiting period' of at least three months. If you are terminally ill, and in some other circumstances however, there is no waiting period.

5 / The amount of universal credit

If both you and your partner have limited capability for work and/or limited capability for work-related activity, you only get one element. You get the higher element that applies. Note that you cannot get the limited capability for work element or the limited capability for work-related activity element in addition to the 'carer element', even if you qualify for both. You get the highest amount that applies. However, if you are in a couple and one of you qualifies for the limited capability for work-related activity element and the other qualifies for the carer element, you can receive both elements.

If you are getting either the limited capability for work or limited capability for work-related activity element and you start work, you do not automatically lose the element, but your capability may be reassessed.

Note: if you are already in work and your weekly earnings are at least 16 times the national minimum wage, you can only be assessed for these elements if you get disability living allowance, child disability payment, personal independence payment, adult disability payment or attendance allowance. In addition, this rule applies if an assessment is to review a previous assessment decision made for employment and support allowance eligibility purposes, or if you can be treated as having either limited capability for work or limited capability for work related activity – eg, if you are receiving chemotherapy).

The carer element

If you or your partner are caring for someone who is severely disabled, you may get an additional amount added to your standard allowance. This is called the 'carer element'.

Monthly rate of carer element, 2024/25	
Carer element	£198.31

You can get the carer element if you are caring for a severely disabled person for at least 35 hours a week. The person you care for must get attendance allowance, the middle or highest rate of the care component of disability living allowance or child disability payment, or either rate of daily living component of personal independence payment or adult disability payment. If you qualify for carer's allowance, which is another benefit for carers, you also qualify for the carer element. Even if you do not get carer's allowance, you can still get the carer element if you care for the person for at least 35 hours a week. This is the case even if your earnings are too high to claim carer's allowance. Only one person can get the carer element in respect of a disabled person, even if more than one person is caring for them.

If both you and your partner qualify for the carer element, you get two elements, but not if you are both caring for the same disabled person.

You cannot get the limited capability for work-related activity element in addition to the carer element. You get the highest amount that applies. However, if you are in a couple where one of you qualifies for the limited capability for work-related activity element and the other qualifies for the carer element, you can receive both elements in this situation.

EXAMPLE

One member of a couple is ill, the other is a carer

Jeremy has cancer and is recovering from chemotherapy. He has been assessed as having limited capability for work-related activity. Laura is caring for him. Jeremy gets personal independence payment daily living component. Their universal credit includes a limited capability for work-related activity element of £416.19 and a carer element of £198.31 a month.

Housing costs element

Universal credit can include an amount for certain housing costs. This is called the 'housing costs element'. The housing costs element can cover your rent and/or some 'service charges'. Service charges are fees such as for communal maintenance and repairs.

The housing costs element usually only covers the housing costs for the home you pay rent for and live in. However, in certain situations, it can be paid for a home you are not living in. For example, if you are disabled and you are waiting for a new home to be adapted, there are limited situations in which you can receive a housing costs element for two homes for up to one month.

If you are fleeing domestic abuse and are living in temporary accommodation but intend to return home, the housing costs element can be paid on both homes for up to 12 months.

Sometimes, you cannot get a housing costs element – eg, if you are paying rent to a close relative and you are also living with them.

If you have a mortgage, you may be able to get a loan from the DWP to help you pay the interest.

Note: if you live in certain types of 'specified accommodation' (including where you get care, support or supervision) or temporary homeless accommodation, your universal credit does not include a housing costs element – you can get housing benefit to help with your rent instead. Chapter 2 explains who is affected by this.

Help with your rent
The amount included in your universal credit to help you with your rent depends on how many people are in your family and on your circumstances.

5/The amount of universal credit

What CPAG says

Discretionary housing payments

If the amount of your universal credit housing costs element does not cover the full amount of your rent, or you are affected by the benefit cap, you may be able to get a 'discretionary housing payment' from your local authority to cover the shortfall.

The Scottish government provides funding through discretionary housing payments to mitigate the effects of the bedroom tax and the benefit cap. This means that if you live in Scotland and are affected by the bedroom tax or the benefit cap, you should get a discretionary housing payment if you apply for one.

If you are renting from a local authority or housing association, the amount of the housing costs element is based on the rent you pay, plus certain service charges. However, the amount may be reduced if you are considered to be living in a property that has more bedrooms than you are entitled to and is considered too big for you. This reduction is often called the 'bedroom tax'. See Box B for how many bedrooms you are entitled to.

Box B
How many bedrooms are you entitled to?

You are entitled to one bedroom for each of the following:

- a couple
- someone aged 16 or over
- two children (under age 16) of the same gender
- two children aged under 10
- any other child
- a carer (or carers) providing overnight care to a disabled child or adult

In some circumstances, you may be allowed an additional bedroom – eg, if you have a child with a disability or if you are a couple but cannot share a room with your partner because of a disability.

If you have one more bedroom than you are entitled to, your housing costs element is reduced by 14 per cent of your rent. If you have two or more additional bedrooms, your housing costs element is reduced by 25 per cent of your rent.

> **EXAMPLE**
>
> **Housing costs element**
>
> Sunni is a lone parent with two children – a boy aged 10 and a girl aged 12. She is allowed three bedrooms under the universal credit rules. Her housing association house has four bedrooms and her monthly rent is £400. Her housing costs element is reduced by 14 per cent of her rent (£56). Her housing costs element is £344 (£400 – £56).

If you are renting from a private landlord, the amount of the housing costs element is limited to the 'local housing allowance' in your area for the size of property you are assessed as needing.

The number of bedrooms you are entitled to is the same as in Box B, except that there is a maximum of four bedrooms.

If you are single, aged under 35 and have no dependants or non-dependants that live with you, you are usually only eligible for a housing costs element to cover the rent for a room in shared accommodation.

Non-dependant deductions

The amount of the housing costs element you get (whether you rent from a local authority, housing association or private landlord) is reduced if you have any non-dependants living with you. A 'non-dependant' is someone, such as an adult child or a friend, who shares your home. A set amount of £91.47 a month (in 2024/25) for each non-dependant is deducted from the housing costs element, as it is assumed that they will contribute towards the rent, even if they do not. There are some situations where no amount is deducted – eg, if you or the non-dependant are getting the middle or highest rate care component of disability living allowance or child disability payment or the daily living component of personal independence payment or adult disability payment, or if your non-dependant is under 21 years old.

> **What CPAG says**
>
> **Deductions for non-dependants**
>
> If you have a non-dependant living with you, check that your housing costs element has been worked out correctly, as sometimes a deduction is made when it should not be.

Help with service charges if you are an owner-occupier

If you own your home, you may get a housing costs element in your universal credit to help with certain service charges. However, you do not get an amount included if you are doing any paid work, irrespective of how few hours you work.

Usually you cannot get any help with your service charges during the first nine months of your universal credit award. You may be able to get help earlier if you were previously getting income support, jobseeker's allowance or employment and support allowance.

If the housing costs element stops being included in your universal credit award (eg, because you have started work) but you remain entitled, you must wait nine months after stopping work before it can be included again.

Childcare costs element

Your universal credit can include an amount for your childcare costs – called the 'childcare costs element' – if you are in paid work (or are about to start paid work) and you are paying for formal childcare, such as a registered childminder, nursery or after-school club. Childcare costs can be paid for a child up to 1 September following their 16th birthday.

You must be:

- a lone parent
- a couple and both of you are working
- a couple and one of you is working and the other has limited capability for work, or is caring for a disabled person or is temporarily away from home

You are treated as working if you are getting statutory sick pay, maternity allowance or statutory maternity, adoption, paternity or shared parental pay.

You can get this element irrespective of how few hours you work. However, the childcare costs must be necessary to enable you to take up, or continue in, paid work or to enable you to maintain your childcare arrangements, allowing you to return to work – eg, after maternity leave.

The childcare costs element in 2024/25 is 85 per cent of your actual childcare costs, up to a maximum of £1,014.63 a month for one child or £1,739.37 for two or more children.

> **EXAMPLES**
>
> **Childcare costs element**
>
> Leila is a lone parent with one child. She is working and has childcare costs of £600 a month. Leila gets a childcare costs element of £510 a month in her maximum universal credit amount – ie, 85 per cent of £600.
>
> Amy and Johnny have two children and both work. Their childcare costs are £1,200 a month. They get a childcare costs element of £1,020 a month in their maximum universal credit amount – ie, 85 per cent of £1,200.

What CPAG says

Advance childcare costs

Some childcare providers require a deposit or advance payment of fees before they will confirm a childcare place. You may not be able to start work until the childcare place is available and you cannot afford to pay for the childcare until you have received your first wages. Even if a childcare provider is prepared to wait for payment, the childcare costs element in universal credit can only be included after you have actually paid the provider. If you need help for childcare before you start work, or before the end of your assessment period, ask your 'work coach' about getting help through the Flexible Support Fund. This is available through Jobcentre Plus staff, and payments are not repayable. If you are refused help from the Flexible Support Fund, request a 'budgeting advance' of universal credit. These payments are discretionary and must be repaid within 12 months. You cannot get a budgeting advance again if you are still repaying an earlier one.

Providing evidence

You must report your childcare costs by the end of the 'assessment period' that follows the assessment period in which you paid them (if later, give your reasons for the delay). You can be asked to provide further information or evidence, usually within 14 days. If you have been asked for proof of your payments but could not provide evidence in time as your childcare provider does not give monthly receipts, and your universal credit award does not include the childcare costs element, ask for a 'mandatory reconsideration' of the decision and appeal, if necessary.

You may be given conflicting information about whether to upload evidence to your online journal, hand it in to the job centre or post it. Any of these methods should be acceptable.

Transitional SDP element

If a 'severe disability premium' (SDP) was included in your (or your partner's) legacy benefit at the time you made your claim for universal credit, you may get the 'transitional SDP element' added to your universal credit award. See Chapter 2 for more information.

> **EXAMPLES**
>
> **Maximum universal credit**
>
> Pamela and Nina are a couple aged 45 and 46 with two children under 10 (born before 6 April 2017). None of the family have health problems. The couple live in a two-bedroom local authority flat with a monthly rent of £450. They have no childcare costs.
>
> Standard allowance £617.60
>
> Child element x two £621.25
>
> Housing costs element £450
>
> Maximum universal credit = £1,688.85
>
> Catja is a lone parent aged 30 with one child (born before 6 April 2017). She lives in a three-bedroom housing association house and her rent is £500 a month. The house has one more bedroom than Catja is allowed, so her housing costs element is reduced by 14 per cent of the rent. Catja's child has a disability and gets the lowest rate of disability living allowance care component. She pays £200 a month for childcare.
>
> Standard allowance £393.45
>
> Child element £333.33
>
> Disabled child addition £156.11
>
> Housing costs element £430 ('bedroom tax' deduction of 14 per cent of £500 = £70; £500 − £70 = £430)
>
> Childcare costs element £170 (85 per cent of £200 =£170)

Maximum universal credit = £1,482.89

Note: in both examples, if the eldest child was born on or after 6 April 2017, the amount of the child element for that child would be reduced to £287.92.

2. How do your income and capital affect universal credit?

If you and your partner have any income or 'capital', your universal credit may be affected. Your income could be your earnings or other income, such as other benefits. Your capital includes savings and some property. As your income increases, the amount of universal credit you get usually decreases.

Income and capital belonging to your children is ignored.

How do your earnings affect universal credit?

Your earnings from employment or self-employment may affect the amount of universal credit you get. Your 'net earnings' are taken into account, which means earnings after deducting tax, national insurance and any contribution to an occupational pension scheme.

Statutory sick pay and statutory maternity, paternity, shared parental and adoption pay also count as earnings.

Your 'maximum universal credit' amount is reduced by a proportion of your earnings. This is often called the 'taper' or work earnings taper rule – ie, the rate at which your universal credit tapers away as your earnings increase. The taper rate is currently 55 per cent. This means that your universal credit is reduced by 55 pence for every pound you earn.

Some people can earn a certain amount (known as a 'work allowance') before their universal credit is affected by the taper rule.

If you have a child, or if you or your partner have 'limited capability for work', you are eligible to have a work allowance deducted from your earnings before your universal credit starts being reduced. The amount of the work allowance depends on whether you have a 'housing costs element' included in your universal credit. A household can only have one work allowance, even if you are a couple and both of you have earnings.

Amount of monthly work allowance, 2024/25	
Universal credit includes a housing costs element	£404
Universal credit does not include a housing costs element	£673

If you receive housing benefit because you are in temporary accommodation and you also receive universal credit, the lower work allowance applies to you.

EXAMPLES

Work allowance

Aaron and Robert are a couple with two children. They have a housing costs element included in their universal credit award. Their work allowance is £404 a month.

Stacy is single and has no children. She has limited capability for work. She has no housing costs element included in her universal credit award. Her work allowance is £673 a month.

Ella is a lone parent with one child. She owns her own home and pays a service charge, but because she is working there is no housing costs element included in her universal credit award. Her work allowance is £673 a month.

How are your earnings assessed?

Your employer is required to report your earnings to HM Revenue and Customs every month. This is called 'real-time information'. If your earnings are reported by your employer in this way, the figure provided in the real-time information report will be used by the DWP to calculate your universal credit. If your employer does not report your earnings in time, the DWP may ask you to give this information instead.

The earnings figure used in the universal credit calculation is the amount you received in each universal credit 'assessment period', which is one calendar month period starting on the date you claim universal credit. This means that your monthly amount of universal credit will change if your earnings go up or down.

> **EXAMPLE**
>
> **Earnings figure**
>
> Kenneth claims universal credit on 8 April. His first universal credit assessment period starts on 8 April. Each assessment period after that starts on the 8th of the month. In the first assessment period (from 8 April to 7 May), he has earnings which are paid on 25 April. This is the earnings figure used to calculate his universal credit for the period 8 April to 7 May.

What CPAG says

> **Two paydays in one monthly assessment**
>
> People paid monthly might occasionally have two paydays in one monthly assessment. If this happens, and your monthly earnings are not automatically reallocated by the DWP to the correct assessment period where it was earned, you should inform the DWP of this by seeking a 'mandatory reconsideration' of the decision that includes two wages in one assessment period.

Are you self-employed?
If you are self-employed, you must report your income and expenses to the DWP every month. There is a special online tool for this. Expenses can include regular costs like rent or wages, purchase of stock and utility bills. Flat-rate deductions are made for some expenses, such as mileage. If you make a loss, this can be carried forward and deducted from any profit made in subsequent months.

If you are self-employed and on a low income, you may be assumed to have a higher income than you actually have. After 12 months of being on universal credit while self-employed, you may be treated as earning at least the national minimum wage for someone of your age for the number of hours the DWP expects you to search for work. This is called the 'minimum income floor' and rather than your actual income, this figure is used to calculate your universal credit. However, if you are not working regularly (eg, because there is little work available or you are unwell), that may indicate you are not in 'gainful self-employment' and you should not be treated as having income that you do not have. Inform the DWP if this applies.

Do you have other income?

Certain types of other income known as 'unearned income' are taken into account for universal credit. For example, the following are considered unearned income and count as income:

- occupational and personal pensions
- state retirement pension
- certain benefits, including contribution-based jobseeker's allowance and contributory employment and support allowance (also known as 'new-style' jobseeker's allowance and 'new-style' employment and support allowance)
- maintenance for you or your spouse or partner, but not child maintenance
- student maintenance loans and some grants
- certain insurance payments
- income from an annuity or certain trusts
- income you are treated as having from capital (see below)

Income (other than earnings) which the DWP takes into account, is deducted from your universal credit in full, on a pound for pound basis.

Disability living allowance, child disability payment, personal independence payment, adult disability payment, attendance allowance, bereavement support payment, war pensions and child benefit are not taken into account as income, nor is income from lodgers.

5 / The amount of universal credit

Do you have any capital?

Any capital you have may affect your universal credit. 'Capital' includes savings, stocks and shares, property and trusts. Certain types of capital are ignored – eg, property that is your main home, personal injury payments placed in a trust fund, some other compensation payments and, for at least six months, your former home that you are trying to sell. Any capital owned by your children is ignored.

If you and your partner have capital of more than £16,000, you cannot get universal credit. The one exception to this is if you move from tax credits to universal credit as part of the 'managed migration' process – any capital you have over £16,000 is ignored for up to 12 assessment periods.

You are treated as still having capital if you deliberately get rid of it in order to get universal credit or to increase the amount of universal credit you get. This does not apply if you have used the capital to reduce or pay a debt, or to pay for goods or services which are considered reasonable.

Is your capital over £6,000?

If your capital is more than £6,000 but £16,000 or less, you are treated as having an income of £4.35 a month for every £250 (or part of £250) over £6,000, regardless of whether you actually receive this income – eg, in the form of interest on your savings.

> **EXAMPLE**
>
> **Income from capital**
>
> Jess has £7,400 savings. This is £1,400 more than £6,000. She is treated as having an income from this capital of £26.10 a month (£4.35 for every £250, or part of £250, over £6,000). This income reduces her maximum universal credit pound for pound.

3. How much universal credit do you get?

How do you calculate universal credit?

Follow the steps below to work out your entitlement. Universal credit is worked out on a month-by-month basis.

Step 1: calculate your maximum universal credit
Add together your 'standard allowance' and any additional 'elements' that apply to you and your circumstances – for example, if you have children, or for other special circumstances (such as the 'limited capability for work-related activity element', 'carer element', 'childcare costs element'), and any 'housing costs element'. You may also have a 'transitional SDP element' or a 'transitional element'. The total is your 'maximum universal credit'.

If you have no other income, this total is the amount of universal credit you get. However, if you are subject to the 'benefit cap' or have any other deductions, the amount you get may be restricted.

If you have other income, go to Step 2.

Step 2: calculate any 'unearned income'
Your income might include other benefits (such as contributory employment and support allowance), an occupational pension or income from capital. Remember that some benefits, including disability living allowance, personal independence payment and child benefit, are ignored. Your income is worked out on a monthly basis.

Step 3: calculate your earnings and check whether a work allowance applies
Calculate your earnings received for the month, after tax, national insurance and any contribution you make to an occupational pension have been deducted. If you are an employee, this is usually the amount your employer reports through the 'real-time information' system, so it is likely to be the same as the information on your payslip. If you are self-employed, you may be treated as having higher earnings than you actually have if you are affected by the minimum income floor.

Check whether a 'work allowance' applies to you and, if so, deduct it from your net earnings.

Calculate 55 per cent of the resulting figure.

Step 4: calculate your total income
Add together the income to be taken into account in Steps 2 and 3.

Step 5: calculate your universal credit entitlement
Deduct your total income to be taken into account (Step 4) from your maximum universal credit (Step 1).

This is the amount of universal credit you get. However, the amount you get may be reduced further by the benefit cap or any other deductions that apply.

> **EXAMPLE**
>
> **Lone parent with two children**
>
> Ashley is aged 30. She lives in a housing association rented property and is not affected by the 'bedroom tax'. Her rent is £480 a month. She does not have any health problems and she is not looking after a severely disabled person. Her two children, who were both born after 6 April 2017, do not have any disabilities. She has no other income apart from child benefit. Her monthly universal credit is calculated as follows.
>
> **Step 1: calculate your maximum universal credit**
> Standard allowance £393.45
>
> Child element x two £575.84
>
> Housing costs element £480
>
> Total = £1,449.29
>
> Ashley has no income apart from child benefit, which is disregarded. She therefore gets her maximum amount of universal credit. She does not need to follow the remaining steps.

EXAMPLE

Couple with one child

Jarbas and Bianca are aged 31 and 32. They live in a two-bedroom local authority flat. Their rent is £300 a month. Their child, who was born before 6 April 2017, has a disability and receives the lowest rate care component of disability living allowance. Their only other income is child benefit and contributory employment and support allowance of £392.17 a month, which Jarbas has been getting since May 2022 because he has limited capability for work. Their monthly universal credit is calculated as follows.

Step 1: calculate your maximum universal credit
Standard allowance £617.60

Child element £333.33

Disabled child addition £156.11

Housing costs element £300

Total = £1,407.04

Step 2: work out your unearned income
Employment and support allowance £392.17 (disability living allowance and child benefit are disregarded).

Step 3: work out your earnings and how much can be ignored
Jarbas and Bianca do not have any earnings.

Step 4: calculate your total income
Their total income is £392.17.

Step 5: calculate your universal credit entitlement
£1,407.04 – £392.17 = £1,014.87

EXAMPLE

Single person

Omar is aged 24. He is single and has no children. He has a disability and receives the standard rate of the daily living component and the enhanced rate of the mobility component of personal independence payment. He has limited capability for work, which began after 3 April 2017. He lives in a housing association flat and is not affected by the bedroom tax. His rent is £400 a month. Omar has net earnings of £416 a month. He has an overpayment of housing benefit. His monthly universal credit is calculated as follows.

Step 1: calculate your maximum universal credit
Standard allowance £311.68

Housing costs element £400

Total = £711.68

Step 2: work out your unearned income
Personal independence payment is disregarded and therefore Omar has no income other than his earnings.

Step 3: work out your earnings and how much can be ignored
Omar has £416 a month net earnings.

The lower work allowance of £404 applies to Omar.

£416 − £404 = £12

£12 × 55% = £6.60

Step 4: calculate your total income
Omar's total income is £6.60

Step 5: calculate your universal credit entitlement
£711.68 − £6.60 = £705.08

Omar has an overpayment which the DWP is deducting this from his universal credit. Therefore his universal credit amount is reduced further.

£705.08 − £23 (overpayment) = £682.08

EXAMPLE

Couple with one child

Saul and Erica are a couple aged 30 and 29, with one child who was born on 5 May 2018. Erica works and earns £700 net a month. Saul gets £598.87 a month contributory employment and support allowance because he has limited capability for work-related activity. Their only other income is child benefit. They live in a housing association house. The rent is £450 a month. The bedroom tax does not apply. They have no childcare costs. Their universal credit is calculated as follows.

Step 1: calculate your maximum universal credit
Standard allowance £617.60

Child element £287.92

Limited capability for work-related activity element £416.19

Housing costs element £450

Total = £1,771.71

Step 2: work out your unearned income
Saul's employment and support allowance of £598.87 counts in full as income.

Step 3: work out your earnings and how much can be ignored
Erica has £700 a month net earnings.

The lower work allowance of £404 applies to Erica and Saul.

£700 − £404 = £296

£296 × 55% = £162.80

Step 4: calculate your total income
£598.87 contributory employment and support allowance plus £162.80 earnings = £761.67

Step 5: calculate your universal credit entitlement
£1,771.71 − £761.67 = £1,010.04

Have you been transferred to universal credit?

If you are getting a 'legacy benefit', at some point the DWP will transfer you to universal credit. The DWP calls this official process 'managed migration'. There is more information about the transfer process in Chapter 2.

If you are transferred to universal credit as part of managed migration, your universal credit may include an additional amount, called a 'transitional element'. That is intended to ensure that the amount you get when you move on to universal credit is not less than the amount you were getting on your legacy benefits.

The transitional element is calculated by comparing the total amount of all your legacy benefits on the day before you became entitled to universal credit (the DWP calls this the 'total legacy amount') with the amount of universal credit you would have been entitled to on the same day (the DWP calls this the 'indicative universal credit amount'). The transitional element is added to your maximum universal credit amount, but the element will reduce over time if your other elements increase (except for the childcare costs element).

If you have certain changes in your circumstances, the transitional element stops – eg, if you stop claiming as a single person and start claiming as a couple.

You only get a managed migration transitional element if you are transferred to universal credit by the DWP as part of the managed migration process, not if you make a claim for universal credit yourself – eg, after a change of circumstances.

When you transfer to universal credit having made a claim yourself rather than under the managed migration process, that is called 'natural migration'. Because you do not get a transitional element under natural migration, you may be worse off under universal credit than under your old benefits, although this depends on the facts in your case.

> Box C
> **Severely disabled people**
>
> If a 'severe disability premium' (SDP) was included in your (or your partner's) legacy benefit at the time of, or within the one month prior to, your universal credit claim and you continued to meet the SDP criteria up to and including the date of your universal credit claim (even if you make a claim for universal credit yourself – eg, after a change of circumstances, not due to managed migration), then you should have the 'transitional SDP element' added to your universal credit award. Broadly, the SDP criteria means you (or your partner) must have been getting a qualifying disability benefit (such as the 'daily living component' of personal independence payment), no one got carer's allowance for looking after you, and you technically counted as living alone. If you receive arrears as a lump sum, it is ignored as your 'capital' for up to 12 months.
>
> The monthly rates of the transitional SDP element are as follows.
>
> **Single people**
>
> If the limited capability for work-related activity element is included in the award: £140.97
>
> If the limited capability for work-related activity element is not included in the award: £334.81

Couples who previously got the lower rate of the severe disability premium

If the limited capability for work-related activity element is included in the award: £140.97

If the limited capability for work-related activity element is not included in the award: £334.81

Couples who previously got the higher rate of the severe disability premium: £475.79

Claimants who are entitled to a transitional SDP element may also be entitled to an extra additional amount if they had previously been entitled to other amounts in legacy benefit which related to either their disability, their partner's disability or their child's disability.

Will your universal credit be reduced due to the benefit cap?

Your monthly benefit entitlement may be reduced or 'capped' to a level set by the government. This is known as the 'benefit cap'.

Benefit cap, 2024/25		
	London	Outside London
Single person, no dependent children	£1,413.92	£1,229.42
Everyone else	£2,110.25	£1,835.00

Your 'benefit entitlement' includes universal credit, child benefit and many other benefits, but does not include pension credit or retirement pension. If your benefit entitlement is more than the cap level, the excess is deducted from your universal credit. If you have a childcare costs element included in your universal credit, this amount is deducted from the excess before your universal credit is reduced. If the childcare costs element is more than the excess, no deduction is made.

Are you exempt from the benefit cap?

You may be exempt from the benefit cap in certain circumstances.

- You are getting personal independence payment, adult disability payment, disability living allowance, child disability payment, attendance allowance, pension age disability payment or industrial injuries disablement benefit.
- You are getting carer's allowance, carer support payment or the carer element in your universal credit.
- You are getting guardian's allowance.
- Your child gets disability living allowance, child disability payment, personal independence payment or adult disability payment.
- You have limited capability for work-related activity.
- You are a war pensioner or a war widow/widower.
- You earn an amount equal to working 16 hours a week at the 'national living wage' converted to a net monthly amount (called the 'earnings threshold').

If you have been working for at least a year earning at least the amount of the earnings threshold and you stop working, you are exempt from the benefit cap for nine months, known as a 'grace period'.

Further information

You can check the local housing allowance that applies to you at lha-direct.voa.gov.uk/search.aspx.

There is more information about universal credit amounts, and how income and capital are worked out, in CPAG's *Welfare Benefits Handbook*.

Chapter 6
Your responsibilities

This chapter covers:

1. What is the claimant commitment?
2. What are you expected to do?
3. Who must look for work?
4. Who must prepare for work?
5. Who must take part in work-focused interviews?
6. Who has no work-related requirements?

What you need to know

- To get universal credit, you must accept a 'claimant commitment'.
- If you claim jointly as a couple with your partner, they must also accept a claimant commitment.
- If you or your partner do not accept your claimant commitments, you are not entitled to universal credit, either as a couple or as a single person.
- Your claimant commitment lists your general responsibilities while getting universal credit. These 'work-related requirements' range from being immediately available for and searching for full-time work to having no requirements at all.
- You can be told to take specific actions by other methods such as a message in your universal credit online journal or by text.
- If you already work but your earnings are low, you may be expected to look for more work or better paid work.

1. What is the claimant commitment?

When you claim universal credit, you must usually accept a 'claimant commitment' before you can get any benefit. Your claimant commitment is an agreement between you and the DWP. It is a record of your general responsibilities, including the 'work-related requirements' you must meet, while you are receiving universal credit. These are usually set after an interview with your DWP 'work coach'.

If you are making a joint claim with your partner, they must also accept their own claimant commitment, otherwise neither of you will get any universal credit. If you are part of a couple but you are awarded universal credit as a single person, because your partner, for example, is a 'person subject to immigration control', your partner does not need to accept a claimant commitment because they are not a claimant.

Your claimant commitment can be be changed or updated if your circumstances change. If it is changed, you must accept the new version to continue getting universal credit.

If you do not agree with the work-related requirements in your claimant commitment, you can ask the DWP to review it. However, while it is being reviewed, you must accept the claimant commitment in order to get paid universal credit. You should also keep to your work-related requirements, otherwise you may be given a 'sanction' and the amount of your universal credit may be reduced.

What does a claimant commitment include?

The claimant commitment sets out what you must generally do in return for receiving universal credit. This includes what work-related requirements are expected of you.

Your initial claimant commitment is usually drawn up by your work coach in a meeting after you claim. It includes the following information.

- Your general work-related requirements.
- Details of specific things you must do, and by when.
- If you must look for work, the kind of work you are looking for, the number of hours you are expected to spend searching for work and when you are expected to be available for work.
- By how much your universal credit will be reduced, and for how long, if you do not meet your requirements and your award is 'sanctioned' (see Chapter 7).
- Details of your right to challenge a decision to sanction your universal credit. Chapter 9 has more information on challenging decisions you do not agree with.
- An instruction to report changes in your circumstances, and what happens if you do not do so.

You can also be required to take specific actions, such as applying for a particular job or attending a course, that are part of meeting your general work-related requirements.

Your claimant commitment does not need to be updated each time you are given one of these specific actions. You should always be given any specific actions in a written form, such as a note in your online journal or an appointment card, so that these instructions can be referred back to if there is any dispute about whether you did the specific actions. However you are told to take these specific actions, you should always be given adequate notice as well as detailed instructions of exactly what you have to do, where you have to go and at what time, and the consequences of not doing the specific action.

If you do not understand anything about a specific action you have been given, you should contact your work coach immediately.

How do you accept a claimant commitment?

The DWP decides how you must accept your claimant commitment. You can be asked to accept it online, by telephone or in person. Usually, the DWP asks you to make an appointment at your local job centre to discuss and accept your claimant commitment once you have completed your online claim.

If you do not accept your claimant commitment within the time allowed by the DWP, you are not entitled and you do not get universal credit, unless the DWP agrees to extend the time limit.

What happens if you do not accept a claimant commitment?

If you do not accept a claimant commitment, you are not entitled to universal credit. If you are claiming universal credit jointly as a couple, each of you must accept an individual claimant commitment. You cannot choose to claim universal credit as a single person if your partner refuses to accept their claimant commitment.

You do not have to accept a claimant commitment if you do not have the capacity to do so – eg, because you have severe mental health problems and someone else (an 'appointee') is responsible for your universal credit claim.

You can be entitled to universal credit without agreeing a commitment in exceptional circumstances – eg, if there is an emergency at home or if you are in hospital.

You must accept a claimant commitment as soon as you can and should explain to the DWP why you could not accept it earlier.

If you do not accept your claimant commitment, you may be offered a 'cooling-off period' (of no more than seven days) to think about this before a decision is made that you are not entitled to universal credit. If you are unhappy with the work-related requirements you have been given, you can ask for these to be reviewed before you accept your claimant commitment. The time limit for accepting your commitment is then extended while it is reviewed.

What CPAG says

Refusing to accept a claimant commitment

If you refuse to accept your first claimant commitment and ask for it to be reviewed, you are not paid any universal credit while it is reviewed. You will only be entitled to universal credit for the period while it was being reviewed if the DWP accepts that your request was 'reasonable'. You must also accept the new claimant commitment that is offered to you or decide to accept the original claimant commitment. The universal credit regulations and guidance do not explain what 'reasonable' means. If you are asked to accept a new claimant commitment when already getting universal credit and you ask for the commitment to be reviewed, your universal credit payments can be suspended while the review is carried out.

Unless your work coach suggests something that is impossible for you to do, it is probably better to accept a claimant commitment and then ask for it to be reviewed after accepting the commitment. This means that you are entitled to universal credit while it is reviewed. Remember that if you do not meet the current work-related requirements in your claimant commitment while you are waiting for your review to be decided, your universal credit may be sanctioned. You cannot appeal against a decision not to change your claimant commitment, but you can appeal a sanction decision.

Can you change your claimant commitment?

In practice, you may be able to discuss and agree changes to your claimant commitment with your work coach. However, the DWP can decide when and how your commitment is updated, even if you do not agree to this. Your commitment may be updated regularly if you must look for work, as you agree different actions with your work coach. You must agree to the updated version to remain entitled to universal credit.

Your claimant commitment must be changed if there is a change in your circumstances that is relevant to which work-related requirements you can be expected to do – eg, if you adopt a child or become entitled to a 'carer element' in your universal credit.

If you are unhappy with what your claimant commitment currently says you must do, you can ask your work coach for this to be reviewed. You must continue to meet your current work-related requirements while the commitment is being reviewed, otherwise your universal credit may be sanctioned. There is more information about sanctions in Chapter 7.

2. What are you expected to do?

Your 'claimant commitment' lists various things that you are expected to do in order to receive universal credit, all of which are designed to help you move into work or increase the amount of work that you do. These are known as your 'work-related requirements'.

There are different work-related requirements – the ones that apply to you depend on your circumstances. You may have to:

- look for work – this involves searching for work and being available for work
- prepare for work
- take part in 'work-focused interviews'

Some people must do all these things; others do not have any work-related requirements at all.

Use the table below to identify which work-related requirements apply to you. **Note**: your partner may be in a different group to you.

If you already work, your individual work-related requirements may be reduced, depending on how much you earn and the number of hours you work. If you do not meet your work-related requirements, your universal credit may be 'sanctioned' and the amount reduced for a period.

Which work-related requirements do you have?

Your circumstances	Work-related requirements
• You are a jobseeker, or you are not in one of the groups below. • You are doing some work, you have low earnings and you are not in one of the groups below.	You have all the work-related requirements.
• You are sick or you have a disability and the DWP has assessed you as having 'limited capabilty for work'. • You are the main carer of a child aged two.	You must prepare for work and take part in work-focused interviews.
• You are the main carer of a child aged one. • You are a single foster carer of a child aged under 16, or the main foster carer in a couple. • You started caring for a friend's or relative's child within the past year.	You must take part in work-focused interviews.
• You are caring for a person with a severe disability. • You are sick or have a disability and the DWP has assessed you as having 'limited capability for work-related activity'. • You expect to give birth within 11 weeks, or you have given birth within the last 15 weeks. • You are the main carer of a child aged under one. • You are the main carer of a child you have adopted within the past year. • You are at least state 'pension age'. • You are a student getting a maintenance loan or grant. • You are a young person in non-advanced education who is 'without parental support'. • You have recently experienced domestic abuse. • You are working and your earnings are sufficiently high.	You have no work-related requirements.

> Box A
> **Main carer of a child**
>
> If you are claiming universal credit as a lone parent, you are your child(ren)'s main carer. If you are a couple claiming universal credit, you must nominate which one of you is your child(ren)'s main carer. Whoever is nominated is then the main carer for all the children in the household. You can change who is the nominated main carer, but usually only once a year unless there is a change of circumstances. If a child normally spends time in both your household and someone else's (eg, their other parent's household), the DWP may need to decide in which household the child 'normally lives' when deciding if you are their main carer.

> **EXAMPLE**
>
> **The main carer**
>
> Matt and Colleen have a joint claim for universal credit. Neither of them work. When their son Charlie is born (their first child), they decide to nominate Colleen as the main carer. She has no work-related requirements, and Matt must look for work. Colleen is offered a job when Charlie is six months old. She cannot take the job unless there is someone else to look after Charlie, so the couple nominate Matt as the main carer instead. Matt no longer has to look for work. Colleen is able to take the job while Matt looks after Charlie.

Who checks whether you are meeting your work-related requirements?

When you claim universal credit, a 'work coach' in your local Jobcentre Plus is usually responsible for making sure you meet your work-related requirements.

The work coach does not make decisions about your entitlement to universal credit; they focus on what your work-related requirements should be and whether or not you have met them. If you are told to do something specific, such as attend a course or an interview, you must be notified in advance, told specifically what you must do, when you must do it and where, and the consequences if you do not do the action.

In the longer term, the main person helping you to look or prepare for work may not be directly employed by the DWP. You might be referred to the Work and Health Programme (in England and Wales), employability support in Scotland (Fair Start Scotland) or another scheme, including an unpaid work placement or a project promoting employment in a particular sector.

Although an adviser employed by one of the schemes could be the person you see most often, all the decisions about your universal credit entitlement, including whether it is sanctioned, are made by DWP 'decision makers'. The adviser may make recommendations to the decision maker, particularly if you have not taken part in a scheme that you received notification in advance to attend.

Proving you are meeting your work-related requirements is mainly managed online, using your online journal, but you may also be asked to attend interviews, and provide evidence and information, to show that you are meeting them.

What CPAG says

Are your work-related requirements too harsh?

You only have the right to have your work-related requirements suspended for a period in very limited circumstances – eg, if you are recently bereaved or if you have experienced domestic abuse in the last six months. However, your work coach has the discretion to reduce the hours you are expected to search for, and be available for, work to what is compatible with, or reasonable in, your circumstances. This includes your long-term circumstances (eg, if you have regular caring responsibilities or a disability) or a short-term situation – eg, if you have a domestic emergency or a sick child. DWP policy is that work coaches should use their discretion appropriately and that claimant commitments should be 'flexible and personalised'.

If you think the work-related requirements in your claimant commitment are too harsh or your circumstances have changed and you should now be exempt from some or all of them, do the following.

- Make sure your work coach or adviser knows about all your individual circumstances that might affect what is in your claimant commitment.

- If your circumstances change and this might affect your ability to meet your current work-related requirements, even if only temporarily, let your work coach or adviser know as soon as possible.

- Ask that your claimant commitment be reviewed if your work coach refuses to change it.

- If you have a good reason for not being able to meet any of your work-related requirements, tell your work coach or adviser as soon as possible to avoid your universal credit being sanctioned.

- If your universal credit is reduced due to a sanction because you did not do something in your claimant commitment or that you were told to do by another form of notification and you think it is unreasonable, challenge the sanction decision.

3. Who must look for work?

Unless you are in one of the groups of people who have fewer 'work-related requirements', to get your full universal credit you must look for work. To be looking for work, you must:

- search for work
- be available for work

You must also take part in 'work-focused interviews' and prepare for work, if you are asked to do so.

What does 'searching for work' mean?

You must usually do anything that is reasonable to help you find work, as well as take any specific actions in your 'claimant commitment' or other forms of notification. The action you take must give you the best chance of finding a job.

> Box B
> **Searching for work**
>
> Work search may include specific activities such as:
> - looking for jobs online
> - applying for specific jobs
> - maintaining an online profile
> - registering with an employment agency
> - cold-calling employers
> - seeking references

When you first claim universal credit, you are usually asked to create an account on the 'Find a job' website, update your CV and create an email address, if you have not already done all these things.

Regular work search activities are then likely to include checking the 'Find a job' website and employment agency websites, contacting potential employers and applying for any specific jobs identified by your 'work coach'.

Keep as much evidence of what you have done to look for work as you can. The more evidence you have, the more likely the DWP will accept that you have been taking all reasonable steps to search for work so your universal credit will not be 'sanctioned'.

You must usually spend 35 hours a week searching for work. However, if you spend fewer hours searching for work in a week, your universal credit should not be sanctioned, provided the DWP is satisfied you took all reasonable action to find work in that week. Some people may be allowed to restrict their work search to fewer than 35 hours a week.

If this is agreed with your work coach, you are only expected to be available for work for the same number of hours. For example, if your claimant commitment says that you must spend 10 hours a week searching for work, you are only expected to be available to take up work 10 hours a week.

You may also be able to restrict your work search in other ways – eg, to the type of work or the location.

You may be able to restrict your work search if:

- you have a good work history (for the first four weeks of your claim)
- you have a health problem or disability
- you are caring for a child or a person with a disability

Do you already work?
If you are working but your earnings are low, you may be expected to search for more work. This could be by working more hours for your current employer, or taking a second job or a different job with better pay. The hours you spend at work plus your travelling time should be deducted from the time you must spend searching for more work each week, provided your work coach agrees it is reasonable to do so.

> **EXAMPLE**
>
> **Searching for more work**
>
> Paul is single with no caring responsibilities or health problems, so he is usually expected to spend 35 hours a week searching for work. He gets a job, working six hours on one day a week. He must drive one hour each way to get to and from work. Although he must still search for more work, he now only needs to spend 27 hours a week searching, as his work coach agrees that it is reasonable for him to deduct the eight hours he spends working and travelling.

Your universal credit can be sanctioned if you do not take up an offer of more work, unless your work coach agrees that you had a good reason for refusing the work. To avoid this situation, make sure you discuss with your work coach any difficulties that taking on more work would cause you before refusing it – eg, if your current job allows you to work flexibly around your caring responsibilities but the new one would not. If your universal credit is sanctioned, you can challenge the decision and argue that you had a good reason, but there is no guarantee that your challenge will succeed.

Who does not need to search for more work?

If you are working and your gross earnings are more than a certain amount, you can no longer be required to search for work (or have any other work-related requirements). That amount is called the 'earnings threshold'.

Your 'individual earnings threshold' is set at the monthly amount you would earn if you worked the equivalent number of hours that you must spend searching for work each week (usually 35, but could be lower depending on your circumstances – eg, children, ill health) and you were paid at the 'national minimum wage' for your age. It is less than this if you are an apprentice. The amount of your individual earnings threshold should be in your claimant commitment.

Unless you have been selected for a 'pilot', the DWP currently uses a lower 'administrative' earnings threshold instead. If you earn above this threshold, the DWP no longer expects you to search for, or be available for, work. However, you may still be expected to take part in telephone interviews, unless you earn over your individual earnings threshold. The DWP calls this the 'light touch regime'. The lower administrative earnings threshold is the amount you would get if you were claiming jobseeker's allowance (plus the 'earnings disregard' that would apply). In 2024/25, this is £892 a month for a single person and £1,437 a month for a couple.

This same threshold applies if you are self-employed and you started your business or universal credit claim within the last year. This is called the 'minimum income floor'. If you have been claiming universal credit and been self-employed for over a year and it is your main occupation, you are treated as earning the amount of your individual earnings threshold (and so you have no work-related requirements), even if you actually earn less. There is more information about the minimum income floor in Chapter 5.

If you live with a partner, in addition to your individual earnings threshold, you also have a 'joint earnings threshold'. This is your two individual earning thresholds added together. If your partner has some work-related requirements but does not have to look for work (eg, because they are the main carer for your two-year-old child or because they have been assessed as having 'limited capability for work'), they have a lower individual earnings threshold.

If your joint earnings are below your joint earnings threshold, both you and your partner may be expected to search for more work. If you earn more than your individual threshold, but your partner does not earn more than their individual threshold, however, your partner may have to search for more work while you do not. If your joint earnings are more than the joint earnings threshold, even if only one of you earns more than their individual threshold, neither of you need to search for more work (or have any other work-related requirements).

If you live with a partner but must claim universal credit as a single person, a joint earnings threshold still applies – it is calculated as if your partner was expected to work 35 hours a week.

EXAMPLE

The joint earnings threshold

Mark and Austin claim universal credit as a couple. They have no children, health problems or savings and they each have an individual earnings threshold of £1,735.06 and a joint earnings threshold of £3,470.12. Their only other income is Austin's wages, which are £1,600 a month before tax and national insurance. Both Mark and Austin's claimant commitments say they must look for more work.

Three months later, Mark finds a job paying £1,900 a month before tax and national insurance. The couple now earn more than their joint earnings threshold between them. Because of this, neither of them has any work-related requirements, even though Austin's earnings are below his individual earnings threshold.

Do you have a good work history?
If you have been in work recently, for up to four weeks after claiming universal credit, you may be able to restrict the type of work you search for. This includes both the type of job and the level of pay. This is at the discretion of your work coach, who must accept that you have a reasonable chance of getting this kind of work.

Box C
Do you have a good work history?

Whether or not you can restrict the type of job you are looking for may depend on:

- the availability of the type of job you used to do
- your prospects of getting the kind of job you had previously
- the length of time you were employed in the same occupation
- how long it has been since your last job ended
- your skills and qualifications
- training you have done for the job

Do you volunteer?

If you are doing voluntary work, the number of hours that you must spend searching for work can be reduced, provided your work coach accepts that your volunteering gives you the best chance of finding paid work. The maximum reduction in hours is 50 per cent of what you would otherwise spend searching for work, even if you spend more time volunteering.

Do you have a disability or health problems?

If you have a disability or a health problem, but you do not meet the conditions for having limited capability for work or you are waiting for an assessment on whether you have limited capability for work, you may be able to restrict your work search. Ask that your work coach change your claimant commitment to reflect this restriction. Chapter 5 has more information about the test for limited capability for work.

You must spend what is considered a 'reasonable' amount of time each week, given your disability or health condition, searching for work. It does not matter if this restriction means that you do not have a reasonable chance of finding work.

If the DWP accepts that your disability or health has a substantial effect on your ability to carry out certain types of work, or work in a particular kind of place (eg, a dusty environment), you do not have to search for this kind of work. You may have to provide evidence of how your condition or treatment limits the type, location or hours of work for which you are searching.

If you are temporarily sick, you do not have to search for work. You can only use this rule twice a year. You can 'self-certify' as sick for up to seven days, and provide a doctor's note for a further seven days after that. If you are sick for more than 14 days, you do not have to search for work if the DWP accepts that this is reasonable. You may be asked to provide medical evidence. If you are sick for more than four weeks, the DWP may refer you for a limited capability for work assessment.

What CPAG says

Work-related requirements while you wait for a medical assessment

Until the DWP decides that you have limited capability for work, you can be expected to search for and be available for work unless your work-related requirements can be reduced for another reason – eg, because you are the 'main carer' of a child under three. This is the case, even if you have 'fit notes' from your GP saying you cannot work. However, your work coach has discretion about what is reasonable for you to do, and the regulations allow them to reduce the hours you must search for, and be available for, work if you have a disability or health condition. You should also not need to search for, or be available for, work during the first two weeks of any period of sickness (up to two times in any 12-month period), and for longer or for additional periods at your work coach's discretion. CPAG understands that the DWP's policy is that work coaches should use this discretion appropriately when claimants are waiting to be assessed for whether they have limited capability for work. If you are in this situation, do the following.

- Self-certify for the first seven days of sickness and provide a medical certificate from your GP for any longer period.

- Ask your work coach to continue to exempt you from searching and being available for work beyond the first 14 days until your medical assessment is completed.

- If your work coach will not exempt you completely after 14 days, ask that they at least reduce your expected work search and availability hours to what is reasonable in light of your disability or health condition.

- If your work coach will not reduce your expected work search and availability to what is reasonable, ask for a review of your claimant commitment and/or make a complaint.

- If your universal credit is sanctioned because you could not meet requirements that were unreasonable, challenge the sanction on the grounds that you had a good reason.

Do you have childcare responsibilities?

If you are the main carer of a child aged three to 12, you may be able to limit your work search to be compatible with school hours (including the time taken to travel to and from school) or your childcare responsibilities if they have not yet started school.

If your child is aged three to 12 and in school, and you would otherwise expect to have full conditionality applied, you can limit your work search to a number of hours that is compatible with the child's normal school hours (including the child's travel time), typically expected to be 30 hours although this could be less depending on your personal circumstances (including the availability of childcare). If you are allowed to limit the number of hours, you do not need to show you still have a reasonable chance of finding a job.

You may also be able to restrict the number of hours you must spend searching for work if you sometimes look after your child who lives with your ex-partner for part of the week, or if your child is 13 or older but you need to look after them, perhaps because they have additional support needs. If the DWP accepts that you have a reasonable chance of finding work, you only have to search for work that is considered compatible with these caring responsibilities.

Do you care for someone with a disability?

If you are caring for someone who is ill or who has a disability, but you do not meet the conditions for having no work-related requirements at all (eg, if you do not meet the definition of 'carer' because the cared-for person does not get a qualifying disability benefit or is waiting to hear about a claim for one), you may be able to restrict your work search. Provided the DWP accepts that you have a reasonable chance of finding work, you only have to search for work for the number of hours that are considered compatible with your caring responsibilities.

Are there any other special circumstances?

In certain circumstances, you cannot be required to search for work (or be available for work). These include if:

- your partner or child has recently died (for up to six months)
- your childcare has been disrupted
- you are carrying out certain public duties

You should explain your situation to your work coach and ask for your claimant commitment to be changed. However, you may still have to take part in work-focused interviews or prepare for work.

In other circumstances, provided your work coach agrees that it is reasonable, your work-related requirements can also be reduced. This applies if:

- you are doing training or other work preparation
- you are sick for longer than 14 days (you must provide evidence of this, if required)
- you are temporarily looking after a child
- you are dealing with a domestic emergency
- there is a temporary change in your circumstances

Even if one of the above circumstances applies, you must still search for work, be available for work and attend a job interview if your work coach thinks this would be reasonable in your particular circumstances. If you do not do so, your universal credit may be sanctioned and your payments reduced. If this happens, you can challenge this decision and argue that you had a 'good reason' for failing to meet your requirements. Discuss your circumstances in advance with your work coach to avoid a sanction.

Have you done everything that is reasonable to search for work?
If your work coach agrees that you have done everything that could reasonably be expected of you in a particular week, you have met your work search requirement, even if you spent less time searching for work than your claimant commitment requires. This may also be the case if you have had a temporary change in your circumstances, such as moving house, a child being excluded from school or an emergency at home, which has meant that you have been unable to spend as long as you should have done searching for work.

> **What CPAG says**
>
> **Hours of work search**
>
> Work coaches have the discretion to accept a reduced number of hours of work search as being reasonable. They should consider your individual circumstances and what actual work search you did in any week when deciding what is reasonable. If possible, discuss your situation in advance with your work coach and try to agree that you will look for work for a reduced number of hours. Remember that if this is not agreed, your universal credit may be sanctioned if you do not stick to the hours of work search in your claimant commitment.

What does 'being available for work' mean?

'Being available for work' means that you must usually be willing and able to take up paid work immediately. This includes attending interviews in connection with obtaining work. You are expected to accept a part-time job if you are offered one, unless you have a good reason for not doing so.

Usually, you must be available immediately for any job that is within 90 minutes' travel time (each way) of your home. You must also be immediately available for job interviews within the same travel time. You must normally take any job that pays at least the national minimum wage for your age.

If you can restrict the number of hours you spend searching for work because you are caring for a child or a disabled person, or you have a health problem or disability, you only have to be available for work for the same hours. If you have a good work history, you may be able to restrict both your work search and availability for up to four weeks. In some circumstances, you do not have to be available for work at all. These are the same as the circumstances when you do not need to search for work.

> **EXAMPLE**
>
> **Restricting your availability for work**
>
> Karen is a lone parent and has a nine-year-old son. She agrees with her work coach that her expected hours of work should be 30 a week to fit in with her son's normal school hours, including the time it takes him to travel to and from school. Therefore, she only needs to be available for work during the agreed 30 hours when her son is at school.

Do you have to be available for work immediately?

You are usually expected to start work or attend a job interview immediately. There are some exceptions to this, but you must still be willing and able to start work or attend an interview at the end of the additional time you are given.

- If you are employed, you must be given 48 hours' notice to attend an interview, and you cannot be expected to take up a different job until the end of the notice period you must give to your current employer.
- If you are doing voluntary work, you may be given up to 48 hours' notice to attend an interview and up to a week's notice to start paid work, if that is considered reasonable.
- If you are caring for a child or someone with a disability, you may be given up to 48 hours' notice to attend an interview and up to a month's notice to start work, if that is considered reasonable.

4. Who must prepare for work?

Some people are not expected to look for work, but must still prepare for a future return to work. That can apply to you if you have health problems or a disability, or if you are the 'main carer' of a child aged two. However, if you are working and earn at least 16 times the 'national minimum wage' for your age, and you do not need to look for work, you do not need to prepare for work either because you no longer have any 'work-related requirements'.

If you are someone who must look for work, you can also be expected to prepare for work. This can include if you are already working, but your earnings are low.

> Box D
> **Work preparation**
>
> Work preparation can include spending a set amount of time on activities including:
>
> - having a skills assessment
> - attending a 'health and work conversation'
> - improving your personal presentation
> - doing training
> - participating in a government employment programme
> - doing work experience or unpaid work placements
> - developing your own business plan
>
> Other activities may be added to the list if your 'work coach' thinks it is necessary.

> **EXAMPLE**
>
> **Preparing for more work when already working**
>
> Silvia works two days and earns £160 a week. She is single, has no caring responsibilities, and she is not ill or disabled. She is getting universal credit and her 'claimant commitment' says she must spend 21 hours a week trying to find another job or trying to get more hours in her current job, but after a few months she has had no luck. She would like to improve her prospects by getting new skills and so agrees with her work coach to do work experience for one day a week while continuing in her current job. Her claimant commitment is adjusted to say she will attend the work experience, continue to work and still search for more work for 14 hours a week.

What do you *not* have to do?

Preparing for work is not the same as searching or being available for jobs. These are different work-related requirements. However, you may be expected to do work experience or a work placement with an employer. If you are caring for a disabled person or a young child, you may need to explain this to your work coach and ask to be given only work preparation activities that are compatible with your caring responsibilities. However, there is no right to this, and if you do not comply with the requirement, your universal credit may be 'sanctioned' unless you can show you had a good reason.

Note: participation in government employment programmes in Scotland is voluntary and so your universal credit should not be sanctioned if you do not take part in one. However, your work coach can still require you to do other work preparation and your universal credit may still be sanctioned if you do not do so.

Are you ill or do you have a disability?

If you are ill or have a disability and are currently unfit for work, tell the DWP. In some circumstances, you can be treated as having 'limited capability for work', but you usually must complete a 'work capability assessment' to decide whether your health or disability is such a serious barrier to work that you are considered to have limited capability for work. There is more about this in Chapter 5.

If the DWP has decided you have limited capability for work, you must still prepare for work if asked to do so. If you are waiting to be assessed, or it is decided that you do not have limited capability for work and you have appealed against this decision, you must usually look for work, but your work coach can reduce the amount of time you are expected to do this search to less than the full 35 hours a week if they consider this to be reasonable.

> **EXAMPLE**
>
> **Preparing for work**
>
> Marshall has bipolar disorder, which affects his ability to work. He is assessed as having limited capability for work but must prepare for work. Marshall used to work in an office years ago, but he is worried that his knowledge of computing will not be good enough to get a similar job when he is able to return to work.
>
> He attends an interview with his work coach and agrees that he will attend a two-month computing course to update his skills. His work coach agrees to help him look for a one-week work placement after the course ends, so he can see how well he copes with being at work.

If you are assessed as having 'limited capability for work-related activity', rather than just limited capability for work, you do not have to prepare for work.

Are you caring for a young child?

If you are the main carer of a two-year-old child, you must prepare for work. Once your youngest child reaches their third birthday, you may also have to search for, and be available for, work.

5. Who must take part in work-focused interviews?

Unless you have no 'work-related requirements' at all, you must take part in 'work-focused interviews'. How often you have to take part depends on your circumstances. If you are told to attend a work-focused interview and you do not do so, your universal credit can be 'sanctioned' unless you have a good reason.

If your only work-related requirement is to take part in work-focused interviews and you work and earn an amount at least 16 times the 'national minimum wage' which applies to you, you do not need to take part in work-focused interviews because you no longer have any work-related requirements.

What happens at a work-focused interview?

Work-focused interviews usually take place with your 'work coach' but may be with an adviser employed by an agency contracted by the DWP. The purpose is to discuss how you can remain in or obtain work, including getting more work if you work already. It is not enough simply to attend a work-focused interview; you must 'take part' in the interview. Your work coach may decide that you have not taken part in your work-focused interview if, for example, you refuse to speak during the interview, only offer one-word answers or are too hungover to focus.

> Box E
> **What is discussed at a work-focused interview?**
>
> Subjects likely to be discussed include:
>
> - any work that you currently do, including self-employment
> - how you can stay in work or increase your earnings
> - your qualifications and training
> - any medical condition or disability you have which may be a barrier to working
> - your caring or childcare responsibilities and how they affect your ability to work
> - potential work and training opportunities for the future
> - accessing help and support to assist you to work

Are you caring for a young child?

If you are the 'main carer' of a child who is one year old, you must take part in work-focused interviews if asked to do so. However, you cannot have any other work-related requirements imposed on you.

> **EXAMPLE**
>
> **Work-focused interviews**
>
> Thiago is the main carer for his daughter Ana. She is one year old and is looked after by Thiago's mother every weekday morning. Thiago drops her off and picks her up, but he is able to work two hours a day during the time Ana is with her grandmother. He thinks that he might be able to work more hours once Ana turns three and he qualifies for a free childcare place. He must take part in work-focused interviews when asked to do so.
>
> Even if Thiago's work coach thinks that he needs to do more to prepare for increased working hours in the future, this cannot be added to his claimant commitment until Ana turns two.

Are you a foster carer?

There are rules for registered foster carers who have a child placed with them. If you are looking after a friend's or relative's child who is 'looked after' by the local authority (often referred to as 'kinship care'), you may be treated as a foster carer under these rules.

If you are a single foster carer or the main carer in a couple, you must take part in work-focused interviews but have no other work-related requirements from your foster child's first birthday until they turn 16.

If your partner is not the main carer, they usually have the work-related requirements that are appropriate for their circumstances.

You must attend work-focused interviews, but have no other work-related requirements, if you are the main carer of a foster child aged 16 to 19 who has extra care needs, or if your partner is the main carer but you both need to care for your foster child because of the level of their care needs. The DWP must accept that it is reasonable for you not to have to look for work, even for a limited number of hours a week.

If you are between fostering placements, you do not have any additional work-related requirements for the first eight weeks after your last placement ended, provided you intend to continue fostering.

Are you looking after a child of a friend or relative?

If you are the main carer of a child of any age whose parents have died or who are unable to look after them, you must take part in work-focused interviews, but you have no other work-related requirements, during the first year after you become the child's main carer. This also applies during the first year of looking after a child who would otherwise be taken into care.

If the child is being looked after by the local authority, you may instead be treated as a foster carer and have no other work-related requirements until they turn 16.

6. Who has no work-related requirements?

In certain circumstances, you cannot be asked to meet any 'work-related requirements' to get universal credit. However, you must still accept a 'claimant commitment'.

If you are working and your earnings are sufficiently high, you cannot be asked to meet any work-related requirements.

Are you caring for a person with a severe disability?

You have no work-related requirements if you get a 'carer element' in your universal credit. You get this if you care for a 'severely disabled person' for at least 35 hours a week, and no one else gets a carer element for caring for the same person. You do not count as a carer under these rules if you are providing paid care or if you are in full-time education.

The definition of who is a severely disabled person is linked to the rate of disability living allowance, child disability payment, personal independence payment, adult disability payment or attendance allowance received by the person for whom you care.

If you do not qualify for the carer element, but you spend 35 hours or more a week caring for one or more severely disabled people, you may still not have any work-related requirements. However, this decision is at the discretion of the DWP. It must accept that it would be unreasonable for you to look for any work at all, even for a limited number of hours.

There is more information about universal credit and carers in Chapter 10.

Are you older than pension age?

If you are older than state 'pension age' (currently around age 66 for both women and men and gradually increasing to 67 by 2028) and you get universal credit as a couple because you live with a younger partner, you have no work-related requirements. Your partner may have work-related requirements. There is more information about older people and universal credit in Chapter 10.

Are you pregnant or caring for a child younger than one?

If you are pregnant and your baby is due in 11 weeks or fewer, or you gave birth within the last 15 weeks, you have no 'work-related requirements'.

In addition, if you are either a lone parent or the 'main carer' in a couple and have a child aged under one included as part of your family in your universal credit award, or you are fostering a child under one, you have no work-related requirements.

If you are a couple claiming universal credit, you must nominate which one of you is the main carer. Whoever is nominated is then the main carer for all the children in the household. Couples with a new baby can therefore nominate the mother's partner as the main carer of all their children, so they can help with childcare around the time of the birth without having to worry about meeting any work-related requirements. You must decide who to nominate from

15 weeks after your baby is born – from this date the mother no longer automatically has no work-related requirements.

You can change who is the nominated main carer but if you want to do so more than once a year, that is at the discretion of the DWP. You should therefore discuss your plans with your 'work coach' in advance. If your work-related requirements are not reduced, you should continue to meet them and ask for your claimant commitment to be reviewed, as otherwise your universal credit may be 'sanctioned'.

Have you recently adopted a child?

If you are the main carer of a child with whom you have been matched for adoption, you have no work-related requirements for one year after the child is placed with you. If you want, you can choose that this period start up to two weeks before the child is placed with you. These rules do not apply if you were a foster parent or close relative of the child before adopting them.

Are you severely ill or have a severe disability?

If the DWP has decided that you have 'limited capability for work-related activity', you have no work-related requirements.

There is more information about the assessment for limited capability for work-related activity in Chapter 5.

Are you a student?

If you are a full-time student eligible for universal credit and you receive a grant, bursary or loan that is taken into account as income, you have no work-related requirements. **Note:** most students are not eligible to claim universal credit.

You have no work-related requirements during the months in which your student income is taken into account when calculating your universal credit award, so you may still have some work-related requirements during the long summer vacation.

You also do not have any work-related requirements if you are a young student in non-advanced education and you can claim universal credit because you do not get any parental support.

Have you recently experienced domestic abuse?

Even if you would normally have to meet some (or all) of the work-related requirements, you do not have to do so for 13 weeks if you have recently experienced domestic abuse. You must no longer live with the perpetrator and you must tell the DWP within six months of the abuse. Within one month of notifying the DWP, you must provide evidence that the abuse is likely to have occurred. This must be evidence from one of a list of professionals, including a police officer, social worker, or employee of an organisation that is in contact with you about the abuse.

You can only be exempted from your work-related requirements once in any one-year period under this rule.

If you are the main carer of a child and would normally have to look for work at the end of this 13-week period, you cannot be required to look for work for a further 13 weeks. However, you can be required to take part in 'work-focused interviews' or prepare for work.

The definition of 'domestic abuse' includes controlling or coercive behaviour or actual or threatened physical, financial, psychological, emotional or sexual abuse, where the perpetrator was either your partner or certain other relatives.

Further information

On gov.uk there is *Advice for Decision Making*, produced by the DWP for its own staff. Chapters J1 to J3 explain the claimant commitment and work-related requirements.

There is more information on the work-related requirements that apply to universal credit in CPAG's *Welfare Benefits Handbook*.

Chapter 7
Sanctions, fines and fraud

This chapter covers:

1. When can your universal credit be sanctioned?
2. When can you get a hardship payment?
3. When can you be fined?
4. What happens to your universal credit after a benefit offence?

What you need to know

- If you do not meet your 'work-related requirements', your universal credit can be reduced. That is called a 'sanction'. The sanction can last indefinitely or for a set period. Your universal credit should not be sanctioned if you have a good reason for not meeting a requirement.
- If you cannot afford to meet your basic needs because of a sanction, you may be able to get financial help called a 'hardship payment'. This usually needs to be repaid.
- If you are overpaid universal credit because you negligently give the wrong information, or fail to provide information without a good reason, you might receive a fixed-rate fine. If what you did was deliberate and dishonest, you might receive a larger fine or be prosecuted for benefit fraud. Your universal credit might also be reduced.

1. When can your universal credit be sanctioned?

If you do not meet a specific 'work-related requirement', without a good reason, your universal credit can be reduced. That is called a 'sanction'. The amount of the sanction and how long it lasts depends on which work-related requirements apply to you and the reason for the sanction.

Chapter 6 has more information about work-related requirements.

There are four levels of sanctions.

A **high level** sanction can be applied to your universal credit if:
- you do not apply for a specific job
- you do not take up a job offer, even if this was before you claimed universal credit
- you give up a job or lose pay voluntarily or because of misconduct, even if this was before you claimed universal credit

A **medium level** sanction can be applied to your universal credit if:
- you are not available to start work or attend a job interview as set out in your 'claimant commitment'
- you are not doing enough to find work

A **low level** sanction can be applied to your universal credit if:
- you do not undertake any of your other specific work search or work preparation requirements, such as updating your CV or attending a training course
- you do not take up a work placement when told to do so
- you do not attend a 'work-focused interview'
- you do not report a change of circumstances that is relevant to whether work-related requirements can be imposed on you
- you do not provide information, complete a task on your online 'to do' list, or attend an interview about your work-related requirements

A **lowest level** sanction can be applied to your universal credit if you are expected to take part in work-focused interviews (but have no other work-related requirements) and you fail to attend one.

> **EXAMPLE**
>
> **Sanctions if you must look for work**
>
> Sabrina lives alone and has no health problems. She gives up her job to look for a new career and claims universal credit. The DWP does not accept that Sabrina had a good reason for leaving her job and applies a high level sanction to her universal credit for 91 days.

> **EXAMPLE**
>
> **Sanctions if you do not have to look for work**
>
> Steven is unable to work because of his mental health problems, but he is expected to prepare for work, including taking up work placements. His 'work coach' finds him a placement that she thinks is suitable. Steven forgets to set his alarm and misses the introductory session. A low level sanction is applied to his universal credit for seven days, plus the time it takes him to start engaging with the placement.

Do you disagree with a decision to sanction your universal credit?

If your universal credit is sanctioned when you do not think it should have been, you can challenge that decision. You may have had a good reason for not meeting a particular requirement. Your work-related requirements may have been unreasonable or you might not have been properly notified in advance about what you needed to do. You can also challenge the decision if you think the wrong level, length or amount of sanction has been applied.

Chapter 9 has more information on challenging decisions. Unlike many universal credit decisions, there is no time limit for asking the DWP to reconsider a sanction decision.

> Box A
> **Good reason**
>
> In most cases, if you can show that you had a good reason for not meeting a requirement, you will not be sanctioned. 'Good reason' is not defined but the DWP should consider all your circumstances, including:
>
> - if there is an emergency at home
> - if you have a health condition or disability
> - if you are homeless
> - if you have transport problems
> - if you have problems with your post or internet connection
> - your reasons for refusing a job – eg, because you have health and safety concerns, or because your travel and childcare costs would make up an unreasonably high proportion of your pay

Special procedures should be followed before you can be given a sanction if you have 'complex needs'. This could be, for example, if you have a serious mental health condition, a language barrier, substance abuse issues, or if you are homeless.

Your universal credit should not be sanctioned if:

- you are made redundant or take voluntary redundancy
- you leave or lose pay as a member of the armed forces, even if you left voluntarily
- you have been laid off or put on short-time working by your employer
- in certain circumstances, you leave a job or lose pay while still in a trial period
- you are involved in a trade dispute
- you leave a job or lose pay, but your weekly earnings do not fall below your 'individual earnings threshold' (see Chapter 6)

How much is a sanction?

If you are sanctioned, your universal credit is reduced by a fixed daily amount until the sanction is over. This fixed amount depends on your age and whether you are single or in a couple.

There is a 'usual' and a 'lower' sanction rate. The lower sanction rate applies if:

- your only work-related requirement is to attend work-focused interviews
- you are aged 16 or 17
- you are the 'main carer' for a child under one
- you are within 11 weeks of when you expect to give birth
- you have given birth in the last 15 weeks
- an adopted child has been placed with you in the last year

Daily rate of sanction, 2024/25		
	Usual rate	Lower rate
Single, under 25	£10.20	£4.00
Single, 25 or over	£12.90	£5.10
Couple, both under 25 (per person sanctioned)	£7.50	£3.20
Couple, at least one aged 25 or over (per person sanctioned)	£9.50	£4.00

These reduction rates apply to all the levels of sanctions described on page 108.

A sanction might mean you are paid no universal credit at all, if the reduction is as much as, or more than, the universal credit you were due to get. A sanction at the 'usual rate' for a single person is the same amount as their 'standard allowance'.

A sanction might mean that you are left without enough money to pay for essentials such as food and electricity. If that is the case, you should apply for a 'hardship payment'.

> **EXAMPLE**
>
> **The amount of a sanction**
>
> Rory lives alone. His monthly universal credit award is made up of his standard allowance and a housing costs element. When Rory receives a sanction for turning down a job offer, he loses an amount equivalent to his standard allowance until the sanction is over. His housing costs element continues to be paid in full. Rory does not have enough income to live on. He does three things.
>
> - He contacts his work coach to explain his reasons for not accepting the job.
> - He asks an advice centre for help challenging the sanction.
> - He applies for a hardship payment.

How long does a sanction last?

Length of sanctions

Level of sanction	Length of sanction		
	First failure	*Second failure within a year*	*Third or further failure within a year*
High level	91 days	182 days	182 days
Medium level	28 days	91 days	91 days
Low level	Number of days from date of failure until date you comply, plus seven days	Number of days from date of failure until date you comply, plus 14 days	Number of days from date of failure until date you comply, plus 28 days
Lowest level	Number of days from date of failure until date you comply	Number of days from date of failure until date you comply	Number of days from date of failure until date you comply

A sanction is imposed from the beginning of the 'assessment period' in which the DWP decides to sanction your universal credit. It does *not* start from the date when you did, or did not do, the thing you are being sanctioned for. That date might still be important for working out the length of a low level or lowest level sanction.

If you receive a low or lowest level sanction, the most important thing to do right away is contact your work coach and agree to comply with the requirement you were sanctioned for, in order to bring the sanction to an end. If you missed a work-focused interview, for example, you should contact your work coach as soon as possible to organise a new appointment. Otherwise, your sanction could end up lasting for months.

> **EXAMPLE**
>
> **Length of a sanction**
>
> Kwame's assessment period runs from the 14th to the 13th of each month. He is single, over 25, and has limited capability for work but is required to do 'work-related activity'. On 10 May he misses a training session his work coach had told him to attend. On 15 May the decision is made to give him a low level sanction. Kwame's work coach agrees that if he attends a different training session on 20 May, he will be treated as having met the original requirement. Kwame ends up with a 17-day sanction (10 to 20 May = 10 days, plus a fixed seven days for a first low level sanction). The sanction runs from 14 to 31 May. When he gets his next universal credit payment, it is reduced by £219.30 (£12.90 x 17). This leaves Kwame unable to pay his bills, so, on the date he gets his reduced payment of universal credit, he applies for a hardship payment.

If your universal credit has been sanctioned for something you did before you claimed, a second sanction should not be for a longer period. The length of sanction also does not increase if another sanction of the same level is applied for something you did within 14 days of the previous 'failure'.

If your universal credit is already being sanctioned and another sanction is applied, the new sanction starts when the current one ends. However, you cannot have more than a total of 1,095 days of sanctions applied to your universal credit at any one time.

It is possible that you might stop being sanctioned, or be sanctioned at a lower rate, if your circumstances change. For example, your universal credit stops being reduced if you are found to have 'limited capability for work' and 'limited capability for work-related activity'.

Shorter sanction periods apply to 16/17 year olds.

2. When can you get a hardship payment?

If your universal credit is reduced because of a 'sanction', or because of a benefit offence, you may be able to get a 'hardship payment'. These are special payments of universal credit which are not offered in any other circumstances. They must usually be repaid through future deductions from your universal credit.

If you have been sanctioned, you can only apply for a hardship payment if your sanction is at the 'usual rate'. You cannot apply for one if your sanction is at the 'lower rate'. See page 111.

To get a hardship payment, you must be unable to meet your or your partner's or child's immediate and basic needs for:

- accommodation
- heating
- food
- hygiene

Before getting a hardship payment, you may need to show that you have tried to access other sources of support, such as help from relatives, but you cannot be made to accept help from a charity such as a food bank. You cannot be expected to borrow money. You should show that you have tried to stop any non-essential spending, but you are not expected to give up things your children need for school or which you need to look for work – eg, phone or internet.

It is important to explain your circumstances when you apply for a hardship payment. The DWP is more likely to accept that you need one if, for example, you have children or caring responsibilities, or if you are ill or pregnant, or if your universal credit has already been sanctioned for some time.

To get a hardship payment, you must also continue to meet your 'work-related requirements'.

You can appeal if you are refused a hardship payment.

How and when do you apply?

To get a hardship payment, you can request one using your online journal or call the universal credit enquiry line on 0800 328 5644. Ideally, you should make the request on the day of your first reduced payment so as to maximise the amount of hardship payment you will receive, but otherwise do so as soon after that date as possible. Hardship payments can not be backdated. You usually need to reapply every month until your universal credit stops being reduced. However, if you apply less than eight days before a pay date and your sanction period continues beyond that date, you should not need to reapply then.

How much are hardship payments?

Hardship payments are paid at 60 per cent of the daily amount by which your universal credit has been reduced. They are usually paid for the number of days between the date you apply and the date you are due to get your next regular payment of universal credit.

> **EXAMPLE**
>
> **How much are hardship payments?**
>
> Catherine is single and aged over 25. Her assessment period starts on the 2nd and ends on the 1st of each month, meaning that her normal payday is the 8th of each month. Her universal credit is sanctioned for 14 days, from 3 May to 17 May. This means that, when she gets paid on 8 June, her award is reduced by £180.60 (14 x £12.90).

> The daily rate of her hardship payments is £3.56 (£180.60 x 12, divided by 365, x 60 per cent). If Catherine applies for her hardship payment straight away on 8 June, she should get a hardship payment of £106.80 (£3.56 x 30 days). However, if she does not manage to apply until 18 June, she will only get a hardship payment of £71.20 (£3.56 x 20 days).
>
> Catherine's next universal credit payment, on 8 July, is not reduced, so she cannot apply for a second hardship payment then.

When do you repay a hardship payment?

Once the 'sanction period' is over, you must usually repay the hardship payment. Your universal credit award will generally be reduced by a set amount each month until the payment is repaid, in the same way as if you were repaying an overpayment of universal credit. There is more information about repaying overpayments in Chapter 8.

Sometimes you do not need to repay a hardship payment, either at all or for a period.

- You can ask the DWP to write off all or part of your hardship payment: for example, because you cannot afford the repayments. The process is similar to asking the DWP to write off a benefit 'overpayment', which is covered in Chapter 8.

- You do not need to repay a hardship payment while you are working and earning at least a certain amount (known as your 'individual earnings threshold').

- If you are working and have been earning at least your individual earnings threshold for a total of six months since any sanctions ended, any hardship payment you have not yet repaid is written off completely.

3. When can you be fined?

There are two types of benefit fines that the DWP can give you while getting universal credit.

- You can be given a fine known as a 'civil penalty' if you are overpaid universal credit because of something that you have done or failed to do.
- If there may be grounds to prosecute you for fraud, you could be offered the option of accepting a fine known as an 'administrative penalty' instead of being prosecuted.

Get advice immediately if you are being prosecuted for benefit fraud, have been offered a fine to avoid the possibility of being prosecuted, or have been asked to attend a formal interview 'under caution'.

When can I get a civil penalty?

You can be given a 'civil penalty' of £50 if you have been overpaid universal credit by more than £65. The overpayment must have occurred because:

- you 'negligently' made an incorrect statement
- you negligently provided incorrect information or evidence
- you failed to report a relevant change of circumstances 'without a reasonable excuse'

In the first two cases, you are not given a penalty if you have taken 'reasonable steps' to correct your error.

> Box B
> **Negligently**
>
> 'Negligently' is acting carelessly, not paying attention to, or disregarding the importance of, anything that needs to be done in relation to your universal credit. It is more than a simple mistake.

If you disagree with the decision to give you a civil penalty, including if you think the overpayment was not worked out correctly, you may be able to appeal.

> **EXAMPLE**
>
> **Civil penalty**
>
> Bobby works part time. His daughter Jasmine attends nursery while he works and he receives help towards the costs of childcare in his universal credit. Bobby decides that he wants to spend more time with Jasmine, reorganises his work and reduces her childcare by a few hours a week. He mistakenly reports the wrong amount of childcare costs for two months. The DWP decides that Bobby has acted negligently, but that the situation is not sufficiently serious to prosecute him for fraud. Bobby's universal credit award is amended, an overpayment of £180 is calculated and a £50 penalty is added to it.
>
> Bobby can appeal against the decision to add a penalty to his overpayment if he thinks he did not act negligently and/or took reasonable steps to correct his error.

Your partner cannot be fined if they were unaware of your negligence, or if they had a reasonable excuse for not providing the information needed.

When can I get an administrative penalty?

If the DWP thinks there are grounds to prosecute you for a benefit fraud offence, you may be offered a fine (an 'administrative penalty') instead. If you accept this fine, you cannot be prosecuted for the same offence but your universal credit can still be sanctioned for a period. While you are sanctioned, you can apply for a 'hardship payment'.

If you accept the fine, you have 14 days to change your mind. If you withdraw your acceptance, the DWP must refund any of the fine you have already paid, but may decide to prosecute you instead.

If you accept a penalty as an alternative to being prosecuted, the amount you are fined is:

- £350 if there has been no overpayment
- 50 per cent of the overpayment, subject to a minimum of £350 and a maximum of £5,000

> **EXAMPLE**
>
> **Penalty instead of prosecution**
>
> Nick claims universal credit for himself and his two children. When the claim is decided, there is no child element included in his award, as the DWP believes the children live with his ex-wife Danielle, who already gets universal credit for them. Nick has not provided any evidence about when the children stay with him. Although no overpayment has been made to Nick, the DWP believes that he deliberately claimed for the children dishonestly in order to get more benefit, and so he could be prosecuted for fraud. Rather than start proceedings, Nick is offered the alternative of paying a £350 fine. He should get advice before accepting this.
>
> Depending on the children's living arrangements, Nick may be able to argue that he can claim for the children. To be convicted, the DWP must prove that Nick knew he was not entitled to amounts of universal credit for them and was acting dishonestly.

How do you pay a fine?

A **civil penalty** is paid back in the same way as an 'overpayment' of universal credit. There is more information about overpayments and how they are recovered in Chapter 8. If a civil penalty is being recovered from you and the decision that you have been overpaid is later changed (eg, if an appeal against the overpayment decision is successful), the DWP must refund any amount of the fine that you have already paid.

An **administrative penalty** can be recovered in several different ways, including through deductions from your universal credit, from certain other benefits, or from your earnings. If you have a joint universal credit claim, the fine is recovered from your joint award. It may also be recovered by other methods (eg, by deductions from other benefits or from earnings) from you or from your partner.

4. What happens to your universal credit after a benefit offence?

If you are convicted of a benefit offence or you accept a fine to avoid possible prosecution, your universal credit can also be sanctioned for a set period of time. This works in the same way as when your universal credit is sanctioned for not meeting your 'work-related requirements'. You can apply for a 'hardship payment' to help you pay for essentials after being sanctioned.

The sanction lasts for four weeks if you accept a penalty instead of prosecution. If you are prosecuted and convicted and it is your first offence, the sanction usually lasts for 13 weeks. If you are convicted again for another benefit offence, the sanction period is longer.

EXAMPLE

Sanction for a benefit offence

Priya accepts a fine of 50 per cent of the amount of an overpayment of universal credit as an alternative to being prosecuted, after it was found that she had not declared the casual work she had been doing. As well as the fine, her universal credit is sanctioned for four weeks.

Further information

The official guidance about sanctions and hardship payments is in the DWP's *Advice for Decision Making* at gov.uk/government/publications/advice-for-decision-making-staff-guide.

There is also more information about sanctions, fraud and penalties in CPAG's *Welfare Benefits Handbook* and at cpag.org.uk/welfare-rights.

Chapter 8
Overpayments

This chapter covers:

1. Have you been overpaid universal credit?
2. What can you do about an overpayment?
3. How do you repay an overpayment?

What you need to know

- If you are paid more universal credit than you should have been, the DWP is allowed to ask for the money back, even if the overpayment was not your fault.

- You can still appeal against a universal credit overpayment if you think you were not actually overpaid or that the overpayment amount is wrong.

- The DWP usually takes deductions from your universal credit to pay back an overpayment, but it can get the money back in other ways too, including from your earnings.

- You can ask the DWP to reduce your repayments, or suspend them temporarily.

- You can also ask the DWP to write off all or part of an overpayment, but it is only likely to agree in exceptional circumstances.

- These are the rules for *overpayments of universal credit*. When deductions are being taken from your universal credit for an *overpayment of another benefit*, the rules can be different.

1. Have you been overpaid universal credit?

If more universal credit is paid to you than you are entitled to, you have been 'overpaid'.

The overpayment amount is the difference between what you were actually paid and what you should have received.

There are many reasons why universal credit might be overpaid, including the following.

- You give the wrong information when you claim.
- You do not tell the DWP about a change of circumstances, or you mention it late.
- The DWP makes a mistake.
- Your employer makes a mistake when it reports your earnings to HM Revenue and Customs.

> **EXAMPLE**
>
> **How can I avoid an overpayment?**
>
> Milton is making a new claim for carer's allowance. He knows this will affect his universal credit, but assumes that the DWP will automatically update things. His adviser explains that, even though both benefits are paid by the DWP, Milton must update his universal credit online journal as soon as he starts getting carer's allowance, to try to avoid getting an overpayment.

The DWP can ask you to pay the money back, even if the overpayment was not your fault and you did everything that was asked of you. In some cases, you may be able to argue that you had a legitimate expectation of the money that you were overpaid, but this can be complex so seek advice.

If the overpayment happened because you gave the wrong information or failed to update the DWP, you might also be given a 'civil penalty'. There is information about this in Chapter 7.

If there is an overpayment on your joint claim with your partner, the DWP can generally hold both or either of you responsible for paying it back. It does not matter who actually got the money.

Note: the rules are not the same for all benefit overpayments. Get further advice if you are dealing with an overpayment of a different benefit (even if it is being deducted from your universal credit).

> **EXAMPLE**
>
> **I'm getting overpaid – should I tell the DWP?**
>
> Alexa's universal credit payments are higher than expected. She notices that she is still getting a child element although she has told the DWP that her son has left home. The extra money is helping her to pay her bills. She asks her adviser what to do. The adviser explains that, when the error is discovered, the DWP will revise Alexa's universal credit award and she will have an overpayment. Alexa will be liable to pay this back even though she provided the relevant information on time. If she later asks to have the overpayment written off, the DWP will consider whether she reported the overpayment as soon as possible.

2. What can you do about an overpayment?

Appeal an overpayment decision

If you believe that you were not actually overpaid, or that the amount of the overpayment is wrong, you can challenge this through 'mandatory reconsideration' and appeal. Chapter 9 has more information about challenging a decision.

The DWP does not stop recovering the overpayment while you wait for the outcome of your mandatory reconsideration or appeal.

Ask the DWP to reduce or suspend repayments

If you accept that there has been an overpayment of universal credit, you cannot appeal against the DWP's decision that you should pay money back. However, you can ask the DWP to make the repayments more manageable by allowing you to pay them back at a lower rate or by pausing repayments for a while. Call DWP Debt Management on 0800 916 0647. These options will generally only be considered if you can show that repayments are causing hardship, so it is a good idea to have information about your income and expenditure, health and wellbeing ready before you call.

Ask the DWP to write it off

You can also ask that some, or all, of the overpayment is written off. You will need to make a written request: send it to Debt Management (C), Mail Handling Site A, Wolverhampton, WV98 2DF and keep a copy.

The DWP has guidance that says it will only consider writing off an overpayment in exceptional cases. It will focus on:

- your household finances – so provide details of your regular income and spending
- your health, and the health of your family members – so provide medical evidence if relevant

The guidance does not say that an overpayment will be written off just because it was the DWP's mistake, but it does say that the DWP will consider how the overpayment happened, and your 'conduct' – eg, whether you contacted the DWP as soon as you realised you were being overpaid.

Make a complaint, involve your MP or consider judicial review

If the DWP does not do what you ask it to, and you think it is not following its own guidance, you might consider making a complaint, involving your MP or getting advice about 'judicial review'. See Chapter 9 for more details.

> **EXAMPLE**
>
> **Overpayments**
>
> Tamar gets a 'childcare costs element' in her universal credit to help pay for her daughter's after-school club. The DWP tells her she has been paid too much universal credit and revises her award. She is told she owes £400, and repayments start being deducted from her monthly payments. Tamar is now short of money and does the following.
>
> - She asks in her universal credit online journal for an explanation. She is told that universal credit was still paying for a breakfast club that her daughter used to attend, as well as the after-school club.
>
> - She checks whether the amount of the overpayment is correct. She discovers that it is too high. The childcare costs included are still wrong. She asks the DWP to reconsider the amount of the overpayment. She plans to appeal if it is not corrected.
>
> - She asks the DWP to write off the rest of the overpayment. She explains how it was the DWP's fault, not hers. She also explains that she has an anxiety condition which has got much worse because she fears losing her job as a direct result of paying back the overpayment. She says she cannot afford to pay her bills as well as pay for travel to work and childcare.
>
> - She also calls DWP Debt Management and asks them to temporarily suspend her repayments. She lists her income and outgoings and explains that she cannot afford deductions from her universal credit at the moment.
>
> - She gets advice from a local advice centre. An adviser helps with her appeal about the amount of the overpayment and helps make her case to have the overpayment written off.

3. How do you repay an overpayment?

The DWP can recover an overpayment of universal credit by:

- making deductions from your benefit
- taking the money from some arrears of benefit (ie, 'back pay') that you are due to receive
- agreeing a repayment plan with you
- making deductions from your earnings
- taking court action against you

The usual way of repaying an overpayment is through deductions from your ongoing award of benefit. This might be universal credit or it might be another benefit. Deductions can be made from most benefits, but not from child benefit or guardian's allowance. The maximum amount that can be deducted from your universal credit for an overpayment is normally 15 per cent of your 'standard allowance'. However, it can be more than this if you have earnings, if fraud is involved or if 'hardship payments' are being recovered. Remember that you can ask to make lower repayments.

If you are employed, the DWP can recover an overpayment of universal credit from your earnings. This is often called a 'direct earnings attachment'. The DWP sends a notice to you and your employer, telling you both how much will be deducted. Normally, no deduction is made if your net earnings are less than £100 a week or £430 a month.

> **EXAMPLE**
>
> **Repaying an overpayment**
>
> Kelly starts a part-time job. Her universal credit award is adjusted. A year later, the DWP decides it has miscalculated her entitlement since she started working. Her award is revised and the amount she has been overpaid is worked out. The DWP decides to recover the overpayment from her earnings because her universal credit award is now very low. Her employer makes the deductions the DWP has requested from Kelly's wages.

> **EXAMPLE**
>
> **Reducing deductions**
>
> Abhishek is having money deducted from his universal credit to repay council tax arrears, a tax credit debt and a universal credit overpayment. The DWP is deducting the maximum from his usual monthly payment. He is left with £251.18 a month. Abhishek asks for lower repayments and provides details of his income and expenses that show financial hardship. His request is accepted and his monthly universal credit payment increases to £284.67.

Further information

The DWP's *Benefit Overpayment Recovery Guide*, containing guidance for DWP staff to follow when deciding how and when to recover an overpayment, is available at gov.uk/government/publications/benefit-overpayment-recovery-staff-guide.

There is detailed information about overpayments in CPAG's *Welfare Benefits Handbook*.

Chapter 9
Challenging a decision

This chapter covers:

1. Can you appeal a decision?
2. How do you complain?
3. How else can you challenge a decision?

What you need to know

- If you are unhappy with a decision about your universal credit, you can usually appeal to an independent tribunal. Before you do so, you must ask the DWP to look at the decision again.
- Even if you cannot appeal, there are other ways that you can challenge the way your universal credit claim has been handled.

1. Can you appeal a decision?

You can appeal most decisions about your universal credit.

First, you should ask the DWP to look at its decision again. This is called asking for a 'mandatory reconsideration'. Try to do this within a month of the date the decision was sent to you. If it has been longer than a month, but less than 13 months, a decision can still be looked at again if there are special reasons to extend the time limit – eg, you find paperwork difficult to cope with because of a health problem. If it has been more than 13 months since you were sent the decision, you can only appeal it in very specific situations – eg, if you think the DWP has made a mistake about the rules or when challenging a sanction decision.

Box A
Requesting a mandatory reconsideration

You can ask for a mandatory reconsideration:

- by putting a note in your online journal
- over the phone
- in person at the job centre
- on paper – you can print a mandatory reconsideration request form via gov.uk/government/publications/challenge-a-decision-made-by-the-department-for-work-and-pensions-dwp or send a letter

To avoid confusion, try to say specifically that you want a mandatory reconsideration.

It is usually best to make the request in your journal, or in writing and keep a copy. If it has been more than one month since you were sent the decision, include reasons for lateness in your mandatory reconsideration request.

If you do not hear from the DWP about your request within one month, follow it up.

When the DWP makes a decision, it should send you a 'mandatory reconsideration notice'. Once you have this notice, you can appeal to an independent appeal tribunal. You can appeal against most, but not all, decisions. Some decisions you cannot appeal against include:

- decisions about when or how your universal credit is paid
- certain decisions about deductions
- a decision about your 'work-related requirements'

If you cannot appeal, you might have other options – see page 130.

You should appeal within one month of being sent the mandatory reconsideration notice, although the time limits can be extended for special reasons. You can make your appeal online at gov.uk/appeal-benefit-decision/submit-appeal. Download a copy of your completed form. Alternatively, make your appeal by post by completing Form SSCS1, which is available from gov.uk/government/publications/appeal-a-social-security-benefits-decision-form-sscs1. Again, it is a good idea to keep a copy.

> **EXAMPLE**
>
> **Disagreeing with a decision**
>
> Nancy gets universal credit. She has mental health problems and has been getting an additional element in her award because she has 'limited capability for work and work-related activity'. At her next medical examination, she is assessed as being fit for work. She receives a decision saying that her universal credit award will no longer include the additional element. Nancy believes she is too ill to work and wants to challenge this decision. She is not sure how to do so and calls the DWP to say she wants to appeal. Because the rules say she must first ask for a mandatory reconsideration, the DWP treats her call as a request for a mandatory reconsideration. The DWP reconsiders the decision and decides not to change it. Nancy can now appeal. She submits her written appeal immediately so she does not miss the deadline, and goes to her local advice centre for help to make her case. Her adviser also helps her to make a complaint about the way her medical assessment was carried out.

2. How do you complain?

If you are unhappy with the way your universal credit claim has been handled, you can make a 'complaint'. You can do this as well as lodging an appeal, or you can do it when an appeal is not possible or has been unsuccessful. For instance, you may want to complain about:

- a delay
- poor advice from the DWP
- your 'work-related requirements'
- your medical examination
- the way the system affects you

If your complaint is about actions taken by the DWP, you should first take this up with the office dealing with your claim. Contact details should be on any letters you have about your claim. If the complaint is about a 'work coach' or work-related requirements, you may find it helpful to speak to the manager of your local job centre.

If this does not resolve the issue, the DWP has a complaints procedure. For universal credit, this procedure includes being able to make the complaint online. See gov.uk/government/organisations/department-for-work-pensions/about/complaints-procedure.

To complain about a medical examination, contact the provider and use its complaints procedure. Medical examinations for universal credit are conducted by the Health Assessment Advisory Service through several providers. You can find the provider for your area, and their contact details, by visiting gov.uk/guidance/find-your-health-assessment-provider.

Once you have gone through all the steps in the relevant complaints procedure, if you are still unhappy with the response, you can take your case to the Independent Case Examiner. This deals with complaints about the DWP and its assessment providers. It can settle complaints by agreement between you and the DWP or the assessment provider, or carry out an investigation and make recommendations about how a complaint should be settled. If you are still not happy, you can contact your MP and ask them to refer your complaint to the Parliamentary and Health Service Ombudsman.

3. How else can you challenge a decision?

Using your MP

If you do not have a particular universal credit issue to resolve, but you are unhappy with the way the system affects you, you may wish to take this up with your local MP.

You can also take up a specific problem with your MP. Usually it is best to do this if you have already tried to resolve the problem directly with the DWP but are still dissatisfied. In particular, it can be useful to ask your MP for help if there has been a delay in your claim being dealt with.

You can email or write to your MP, or go to a local 'surgery' – ie, the regular sessions that MPs usually have to meet their constituents.

Using judicial review

'Judicial review' is a legal route for challenging decisions by the DWP where appeal is not an option, or is taking too long. It can usually only be used as a last resort. You do not need to be a lawyer to consider judicial review. See cpag.org.uk/jr.

Further information

For information and tactical tips on appeals, see CPAG's guide *Winning Your Benefit Appeal: what you need to know*.

To find out who your MP is and how to contact them, see parliament.uk. You can also find contact details in your local library or town hall, or you can write to your local MP at the House of Commons, London SW1A 0AA.

Independent Case Examiner
PO Box 209
Bootle L20 7WA
Tel: 0800 414 8529
NGT text relay: 18001 then 0800 414 8529
email: ice@dwp.gov.uk
gov.uk/government/organisations/independent-case-examiner

Parliamentary and Health Service Ombudsman
Millbank Tower
21 Millbank
London SW1P 4QP
Tel: 0345 015 4033
ombudsman.org.uk

Chapter 10
Universal credit and specific groups of people

This chapter covers:

1. Lone parents
2. Families with three or more children
3. Carers
4. People with an illness or disability
5. Young people
6. Older people
7. People from abroad

What you need to know

- Almost anyone of working age can claim, provided they meet the basic rules of entitlement and the financial conditions.
- Your personal or family circumstances determine how much universal credit you get and what 'work-related requirements' you must meet.
- There are special rules that allow some 16/17 year olds, and some people over pension age in 'mixed-age couples', to claim universal credit.
- Certain people from abroad are excluded from universal credit.

1. Lone parents

Can lone parents claim universal credit?

Lone parents can claim universal credit.

You are a lone parent if you are responsible for a child who normally lives with you and you do not have a partner living with you.

If you are a lone parent, you make a single claim for universal credit. It is important to be clear about whether you are a lone parent and be aware that if a partner moves in with you, even if they are not your child's parent, you become a couple and must make a joint claim for universal credit.

Are there any special rules?

There is no additional amount of universal credit specifically for lone parents.

If you share the care of your children with a former partner, it is not possible to split payments for children. You can agree who should claim for your child or, if you cannot agree, the DWP decides which one of you has the main responsibility. This does not automatically go to whoever claimed universal credit first, or who gets child benefit, but takes into account a range of factors.

If it is decided that you do not have main responsibility for any children, you are not treated as a parent for the purposes of universal credit. This means you are not entitled to child elements and you must meet the 'work-related requirements' that apply to your other circumstances. The amount you can get to help with your rent may also be reduced if you have a spare bedroom for your child to stay with you.

What are your work-related requirements?

As a lone parent, your work-related requirements depend on the age of your youngest child.

Box A
The work-related requirements for lone parents

- If you have a child under the age of one, you have no work-related requirements.

- If you have a child aged one, you must attend 'work-focused interviews', usually every three months.

- If you have a child aged two, you must attend work-focused interviews, usually every month, and prepare for work. This involves undertaking activity that makes it more likely that you will return to work in the future.

- Once your youngest child is aged from three to 12, you must search for work and be available to take up a job, although you can place restrictions on the type of work and hours you are prepared to do. Your maximum expected hours to look for work is 30 a week, but this could be lower, as it should be compatible with your childcare responsibilities, taking into account your child's school hours, including travel. The availability of childcare should also be taken into consideration.

- Once your youngest child is aged 13, your maximum expected hours to look for work is increased to 35 a week, but this should be compatible with your caring responsibilities, so could be lower.

- Most people are required to attend an interview or take up a job immediately. As a lone parent, you may be allowed up to one month's notice to take up work or 48 hours' notice to attend an interview, taking into account how long you need to arrange childcare.

You may have fewer work-related requirements if you have experienced domestic abuse, or if your partner or child has died, within the previous six months. Your requirements may also be relaxed in other temporary circumstances or if your usual childcare arrangements are disrupted. Chapter 6 has more information on work-related requirements.

> **EXAMPLE**
>
> **Work-related requirements**
>
> Yuka is a lone parent with one child aged six. She gets universal credit and must search for work and be available for work. Her 'claimant commitment' allows her to restrict her availability to school hours during term time only. She is asked to attend a skills assessment course for two weeks while her child is at school. If she refuses to go, she is likely to be given a 'sanction' and the amount of her universal credit reduced. She is offered a temporary job of four hours a day during school hours, every weekday. If she does not accept the job, she may receive a sanction. The job continues to be available during the school holidays. Yuka can get help with up to 85 per cent of her childcare costs in her universal credit, so she can continue working. If suitable childcare is not available, she should not get a sanction for giving up the job.

Do you have childcare costs?

Universal credit can include an amount to help with your childcare costs (a 'childcare costs element') if you are working and paying a registered childcare provider, such as a childminder, nursery or after-school club. There is no minimum number of hours you must work to qualify for help with childcare – any work can qualify, provided the amount of childcare is not considered excessive in relation to how many hours you work.

The full costs of your childcare are not covered. Universal credit will pay up to 85 per cent of those costs with a maximum payment of £1,014.63 a month for one child or £1,739.37 for two or more children. Remember that this amount can be reduced by your income, like the rest of your universal credit. See Chapter 5 for more information on how universal credit is calculated.

Usually universal credit does not pay you in advance for your upcoming childcare costs. Instead, it reimburses you for childcare costs you have already paid. However, if you are starting work or increasing your hours, you may be able to get help from the 'Flexible Support Fund' to pay for your childcare costs upfront. Use your journal or ask your 'work coach' to check whether you may be eligible for this assistance.

Universal credit cannot generally help with childcare costs that have been paid or reimbursed by someone else (eg, your employer) or covered by other support, but you can claim back the childcare costs that were covered by the Flexible Support Fund.

You must generally report your childcare costs in the 'assessment period' in which you paid them, or the following assessment period. If you report them late, they are only included in your universal credit if you have a good reason for the delay.

Are there other benefits for lone parents?

- You should claim **child benefit** for your children, as well as universal credit. There is no limit on how many children you can get child benefit for.

- Lone parents who have been bereaved can claim **bereavement support payment**. Bereavement support payment is not taken into account as income when your universal credit is assessed.

- In England and Wales, you can get a **Sure Start maternity grant** if you get universal credit. This is £500 to help with the costs of a new baby, but it is usually only payable for your first child. It does not matter about other income or whether you are in work, provided you are entitled to universal credit.

- In Scotland, you can get a **Best Start grant** if you get universal credit. For a new baby, this is £754.65 for your first child or £377.35 if you have another child younger than 16 living with you. As long as you are still entitled to universal credit, you will then get an early learning payment of £314.45 when your child is aged from two to three and a half, and a school-age payment of £314.45 when your child is able to start school.

- If you are pregnant or have a child under four years old, you get universal credit, and your take-home pay is £408 or less a month, you qualify for a **Healthy Start card** to help pay for milk, fruit and vegetables, and free vitamins. In Scotland, you can get the **Best Start foods payment card** if you are pregnant or if you have a child under three years old and you get universal credit, regardless of your income.

2. Families with three or more children

Can families with three or more children claim universal credit?

You can claim universal credit if you have three or more children, but you may not be able to get a 'child element' included for a third or subsequent child born on or after 6 April 2017. That is known as the 'two-child limit'.

You can get a child element for all children born before 6 April 2017. You may be able to get a child element for a third or subsequent child born on or after 6 April 2017 if an exception applies. The order of children (ie, whether a child is your first, second or third child) is decided by their date of birth, with the earliest first.

Are there any special rules?

Even if you cannot have a child element included in your universal credit award for a third or subsequent child, you can still have an additional amount included for that child if they are disabled. You can also get help with your childcare costs for that child. There are also exceptions to the two-child limit.

Box B
Exceptions to the two-child limit

- **Multiple births.** If you already have two or more children in your household, then have a multiple birth, you get a child element for all but one of the new children. If you have one child and then have a multiple birth, you get a child element for all the children. If you have no other children and have a multiple birth, you get a child element for all the children.

- **Adopted children.** Many adopted children are not counted towards the two-child limit. However, they still count towards the limit if their adoptive parent, or one of them, had previously been their legal parent or step-parent, or if they have been adopted from abroad.

- **Friend and family carers.** If you look after a child under a formal caring arrangement or informally and the child would otherwise be 'looked after' by a local authority, that child is not counted towards the two-child limit.

- **Children of under 16 year olds.** If a young person under 16 in your household becomes a parent and you are responsible for the new child who is a third or subsequent child in your household, the new child is not affected by the two-child limit.

- **Non-consensual conception.** If you have a third or subsequent child who is likely to have been conceived as a result of rape or in a 'controlling or coercive relationship', that child is not affected by the two-child limit. For this rule to apply, you must not be living at the same address as the alleged perpetrator and you must provide a form completed by a health professional, social worker or other approved person. There does not need to be a criminal conviction, but you don't need a form from a professional if you have evidence of such a conviction or a criminal injuries compensation award.

> **EXAMPLES**
>
> **The two-child limit**
>
> Vanessa gets universal credit and has two children. She gives birth to twins on 30 June 2024. A child element is not paid for the first twin, but it is paid for the other twin. Vanessa's universal credit award now includes three child elements in total.
>
> Sergio and Amanda get universal credit. Their first birth child, Ralf, is born in 2014. They then become legal guardians for Amanda's niece, Emilia, in May 2017, after Amanda's sister dies. In July 2024, Amanda gives birth to another child, Lucas. Because they are legal guardians for Emilia, she is not counted for the purposes of the two-child limit. Sergio and Amanda have three child elements included in their universal credit award.

3. Carers

Can carers claim universal credit?

Carers can claim universal credit.

Are there any special rules?

You can get a 'carer element' included in your universal credit if you care for a severely disabled person for at least 35 hours a week and you are not paid to provide care. To be recognised as severely disabled, the person you look after must get:

- the middle or highest rate of the 'care component' of disability living allowance
- the middle or highest rate of the care component of child disability payment in Scotland
- either rate of the 'daily living component' of personal independence payment
- either rate of the daily living component of adult disability payment in Scotland

- either rate of attendance allowance
- either rate of pension age disability payment in Scotland (being rolled out from October 2024 to April 2025)

You can get a carer element whether or not you get carer's allowance (or carer support payment in Scotland).

Before applying, bear in mind that getting a carer element in your universal credit could mean that the person you care for gets less benefit. This is because they might be getting a 'severe disability premium' in their benefit, and this premium stops if the person who cares for them claims carer's allowance, carer support payment or the carer element of universal credit. Get advice about this possibility before you claim.

If more than one person is caring for the same disabled person, the carer element can only be paid to one of you. If you are in a couple and you are both carers, you can get two carer elements, but you must be looking after different people.

If you are a carer with your own health problems or disability, you cannot get the carer element at the same time as getting a 'limited capability for work' or 'limited capability for work-related activity' element. If you are a disabled carer, make this clear on your claim – the DWP must award the element with the highest value. If you are in a couple, it is possible for one of you to get a carer element and for the other to get a limited capability for work or limited capability for work-related activity element.

> **EXAMPLE**
>
> **Carers**
>
> Maria and Tom care for their daughter who gets the middle rate care component of disability living allowance. Maria works and Tom has limited capability for work-related activity.
>
> Although both Maria and Tom are carers, they nominate Maria as the main carer. Their 'work coach' is satisfied that she spends at least 35 hours a week looking after their daughter, which she fits in around her working hours. Their universal credit award includes the carer element for Maria and the limited capability for work-related activity element for Tom.
>
> If they had nominated Tom as the main carer, their award would only have included the limited capability for work-related activity element, because Tom could not receive the carer element as well.

Unlike carer's allowance or carer support payment, you do not lose the carer element when you earn more than a certain amount (the weekly limit for carer's allowance and carer support payment is £151 in 2024/25). However, if you are in work, your earnings affect the amount of universal credit you get, in the same way as for other claimants. There is no extra 'work allowance' for carers.

Box C
Foster carers

- Foster carers who are legally approved to look after a child or young person by arrangement with a local authority or voluntary organisation are treated differently from other kinds of carers.
- There are special rules for foster carers in universal credit.
- In Scotland, kinship carers of looked after children are treated in the same way as foster carers.
- Lone foster carers are only required to attend 'work-focused interviews'. They do not have any other 'work-related requirements' until their youngest foster child reaches 16 years old, which is when they are required to look for, and be available for, work.
- In exceptional circumstances, when a foster child who is 16 or 17 needs full-time care, the foster carer is only required to participate in work-focused interviews and has no other work-related requirements, until the child reaches 18 or the placement ends.
- Fostering couples must say which one of them is the lead carer. The lead carer is only required to attend work-focused interviews and has no other work-related requirements. The other member of the couple has all the work-related requirements that apply in their circumstances, unless there are exceptional circumstances and the foster child needs full-time care by two adults.
- Fostering is not treated as being self-employed or in work.
- Fostering payments are not taken into account as earnings or income. There is no additional amount in universal credit for being a foster carer.

> **What CPAG says**
>
> **Carers not getting carer's allowance**
>
> It is generally a good idea to claim carer's allowance or carer support payment as well as the carer element of universal credit, even if, because of the way universal credit is calculated, you will be financially no better off.
>
> This is because being in receipt of carer's allowance can help you gain future entitlement to certain contribution-based benefits. Some claimants will also find the more frequent payments useful for budgeting purposes.
>
> If you have declared that you are a carer but have not been awarded the carer element, request a 'mandatory reconsideration' and appeal if necessary.

What are your work-related requirements?

Carers who spend at least 35 hours a week caring for a severely disabled person do not have any work-related requirements, so you can get universal credit without being expected to look for work.

If you do not qualify for a carer element, you may also have no work-related requirements in the following circumstances.

- You care for more than one severely disabled person and your total caring responsibilities amount to at least 35 hours a week.

- You care for a severely disabled person for at least 35 hours a week, but you are not the main carer – eg, because someone else gets a carer element for looking after them.

In these two situations, the DWP must be satisfied that it is unreasonable to expect you to look for work, even within agreed limits.

If you are a carer who does not qualify for the carer element of universal credit, you are expected to look for work. This might be the case if the person you care for is waiting to hear about a disability benefit claim, or has not been awarded a disability benefit, or if they have another carer who claims for looking after them.

Despite being expected to look for work, you should be able to restrict the hours you are available for, and searching for, work to be compatible with your caring responsibilities. However, you will need the agreement of your work coach and you must still have a reasonable chance of finding work. Chapter 6 has more information about work-related requirements.

> **EXAMPLE**
>
> **Carers**
>
> Oscar looks after his brother, who gets the daily living component of personal independence payment. Oscar gets universal credit and has no work-related requirements. His brother's personal independence payment stops following a review. Oscar no longer meets the conditions for the carer element of universal credit, so must now meet work-related requirements. His work coach is satisfied that his brother still has a disability and so he is able to agree some restrictions in his claimant commitment on his hours of availability for work and the notice required to attend an interview or take up a job. Oscar must still show that he is taking all reasonable action to find work within the agreed restrictions, otherwise he may be given a sanction and the amount of his universal credit may be reduced.

Are there other benefits for carers?

Carers can claim **carer's allowance**. In Scotland, this is being replaced by **carer support payment**. To get either, you must spend at least 35 hours a week looking after a 'severely disabled' person – ie, a person who gets one of the benefits listed on p140. You cannot get carer's allowance or carer support payment if you earn more than £151 a week (in 2024/25). If you are a full-time student you cannot get carer's allowance, but you can get carer support payment in Scotland.

Carer's allowance and carer support payment reduce universal credit pound for pound. However, it is still a good idea to claim one of these alongside the carer element, where possible.

In Scotland, if you get carer's allowance or carer support payment, you can also get a **carer's allowance supplement**. If you are aged 16 to 18 and don't get carer's allowance, you may be able to get a **young carer grant** from Social Security Scotland.

4. People with an illness or disability

Can people with disabilities or ill health claim universal credit?

People with an illness or disability can claim universal credit.

> **What CPAG says**
>
> **Claiming online**
>
> If you cannot claim online because of your illness or disability, official guidance says that a home visit can be arranged by the DWP or, in exceptional cases, your claim can be taken by telephone. However, in practice, this is often difficult – you or your adviser or advocate must be very persistent and explain your difficulties in detail in order to get the DWP to agree. If you need a British Sign Language interpreter at an interview, this must be arranged.

Are there any special rules?

There are special rules for some people with an illness or disability. These affect how much universal credit you get, what kind of 'work-related requirements' you have and, if you work, how much you can earn before your universal credit is affected.

Universal credit includes additional amounts for adults who have 'limited capability for work and work-related activity', for health or disability reasons.

Universal credit also includes additional amounts for ill or disabled children, paid at one of two rates, depending on the amount of disability benefit that a child gets.

> **What CPAG says**
>
> **Waiting for a medical assessment**
>
> If you have claimed universal credit as someone whose ability to work is limited by your health or disability, you will usually be asked to complete a health-based questionnaire and take part in a medical assessment. A medical assessment should be carried out within three months of your claim starting but may take longer. You have work-related requirements while you are waiting to be assessed. However, your 'work coach' has the discretion to relax these during this period: ask them to do so, and make sure you provide details and evidence about your disability or health condition and how it affects you.
>
> If your income is too high to qualify for universal credit unless you are awarded the 'limited capability for work-related activity element', you should be awarded a token amount of one penny a month until the assessment is carried out.

Note: if you are found to have 'limited capability for work' (and not limited capability for work-related activity), you cannot get an additional element paid as part of your universal credit unless your period of limited capability for work started before 3 April 2017. However, it is still worthwhile to have this status – it means you get a 'work allowance' and your work-related requirements are less (you only need to prepare for work, rather than look for work).

If you have a disability or health condition and you are also a carer, you cannot get an additional amount for your 'work capability' as well as a 'carer element' in your universal credit. However, if you are in a couple, it is possible for one of you to get a limited capability for work or a limited capability for work-related activity element and the other to get a carer element.

There is more information on the additional amounts in Chapter 5.

What CPAG says

Are you worse off on universal credit?

Many ill and disabled people are worse off on universal credit than they were on the 'legacy benefits'. This is because universal credit does not have some of the 'disability premiums' that could be included in older benefits, and because amounts for some disabled children are lower on universal credit than they were in child tax credit. However, in some cases you can get 'transitional protection' to make sure that you do not lose out when moving from older benefits to universal credit.

It is important to get independent advice before claiming universal credit, particularly if you are claiming before you are asked to do so under 'managed migration'. Chapter 2 has more information on moving to universal credit and transitional protection.

Are you working?

You qualify for a work allowance if you or your partner have been assessed as having limited capability for work or limited capability for work-related activity. This means that you can earn up to a certain amount each month before your earnings start being taken into account in calculating your universal credit. Chapter 5 has more details about work allowances.

There is no rule to prevent you from working while you are assessed as having limited capability for work or limited capability for work-related activity, but the fact that you are managing to work might lead to you being reassessed.

If you become ill or disabled while you are in work, and your monthly earnings remain at least 16 times the 'national minimum wage' a week, you can only have a new 'work capability assessment' for universal credit if you already get disability living allowance, personal independence payment, or child disability payment or adult disability payment in Scotland.

> **EXAMPLE**
>
> **Working with a disability or ill health**
>
> Nicole is a single person who has previously been in good health, working 20 hours a week on the minimum wage. She gets universal credit, but is expected to look for better paid work or more hours. She is diagnosed with a long-term health condition and believes that this is affecting her ability to work. She does not want to give up her job, but feels that she should be entitled to additional support through universal credit as a disabled worker. She asks to be assessed for limited capability for work, which would allow more of her earnings to be ignored, and she would not have to look for more work. Her request is refused because she is already earning more than 16 times the national minimum wage a week. She must therefore first apply for personal independence payment. If this is awarded, she can then be assessed as having limited capability for work for universal credit.

Are there other benefits for people with disabilities or ill health?

You can claim **contributory employment and support allowance** if you are unable to work, and have worked in the past and paid enough national insurance contributions. Payment is limited to one year unless you are assessed as having limited capability for work-related activity, in which case it can be paid indefinitely. You can get contributory employment and support allowance at the same time as universal credit, but it counts in full as income, so reduces your universal credit pound for pound. In some situations, you can get contributory employment and support allowance if you cannot get universal credit – eg, because your savings are too high.

You can claim **personal independence payment, or adult disability payment in Scotland,** if you have a disability or health condition that affects your mobility or ability to carry out daily living activities. If you are over state pension age, you can instead claim **attendance allowance,** or **pension age disability payment** in Scotland (being introduced between October 2024 and April 2025). If your child (aged under 16) is disabled, you can claim **disability living allowance, or child disability payment in Scotland**, for them. These benefits are not affected by, or counted as, income for universal credit.

5. Young people

Can young people claim universal credit?

In general, you must be at least 18 years old to claim universal credit. However, there are special rules that allow some young people aged 16 and 17 to claim.

If you are under 16, you cannot claim universal credit.

Are there any special rules?

If you are aged 16 or 17, you can claim universal credit if:

- you have a child or are about to have a baby
- you are 'without parental support'
- you are disabled or ill
- you are a carer

Chapter 3 explains more about when you can claim in these situations.

If you are a care leaver aged 16 or 17, you cannot usually get universal credit and the local authority still has a duty to support you. You can only get universal credit as a care leaver if you have 'limited capability for work' or you are responsible for a child.

If you are 18 or over, there are no special rules. However, if you are still in education, you may not be able to get universal credit. There is more information about claiming universal credit while in education in Chapter 3.

If you are under 25, you have a lower 'standard allowance' of universal credit than people aged 25 and over. Your age can also affect how much help you can get towards your housing costs. There is more information about how universal credit is calculated in Chapter 5.

> **EXAMPLE**
>
> **Young person estranged from parents**
>
> Natalie is aged 17 and has left school and started work. She has an argument with her parents and leaves home. She finds a room in private rented accommodation, and claims universal credit. She is below the normal qualifying age of 18, and must make a statement explaining that she is estranged from her parents. The DWP looks at her statement and its own guidance, which says there is no requirement to corroborate such evidence or contact her parents. Natalie should be believed, unless her statement is self-contradictory or improbable.

Are there other benefits for young people?

There are not many other benefits that young people aged 16 or 17 can claim for themselves. If you have a health condition or disability, you may be able to claim **personal independence payment, or adult disability payment in Scotland.** If you are a carer, you may be able to claim **carer's allowance, or carer support payment in Scotland.**

In Scotland, you can get a **young carer grant** if you aren't already receiving carer's allowance or carer support payment. Most young people cannot qualify for 'contributory benefits', such as contribution-based jobseeker's allowance or contributory employment and support allowance, because in order to get these benefits you need to have worked and paid enough national insurance contributions, usually for two to three years before you claim.

6. Older people

Can older people claim universal credit?

People older than 'pension age' cannot usually get universal credit and can claim pension credit instead. Pension age is currently 66 for both men and women, and is gradually rising to 67 by 2028.

If you are single, you cannot stay on universal credit when you reach pension age – your universal credit stops at the end of the 'assessment period' during which you reach pension age.

If you are in a couple already getting universal credit, when one of you reaches pension age your universal credit can continue until you both reach pension age.

If you are in a couple not already receiving universal credit and one of you has reached pension age but the other has not, get independent advice about whether you can claim universal credit or pension credit. See the 'What CPAG says' box below.

If you have reached pension age and are getting pension credit as a single person, and a partner under pension age moves in with you, your pension credit (and housing benefit if you are getting it) ends and you must claim universal credit as a couple.

You cannot get both pension credit and universal credit at the same time, and you cannot make two separate claims if you are a couple.

What CPAG says

Mixed-age couples

You cannot usually make a new claim for pension credit if your partner is under pension age. However, if you were already getting pension credit as a couple before 15 May 2019, you can stay on it, even while one of you is under pension age. If one of you reached pension age before 15 May 2019, you can still make a new claim for pension credit if you have been entitled to housing benefit in the same couple since before 15 May 2019 (and you are not on income support, income-based jobseeker's allowance, income-related employment and support allowance or universal credit).

If you are in a 'mixed-age' couple and are being told you need to claim universal credit for the first time, it is a good idea to get independent advice.

If you are getting working tax credits while over pension age, you may be entitled to universal credit. The basic condition to be under pension age is waived in this case, but only if you are notified to claim universal credit and do so before the deadline. You can stay on universal credit as long as you are working but if you stop working you may be better off claiming pension credit and should seek advice.

Are there any special rules?

There is no additional amount for older people in universal credit.

If you are claiming universal credit as a couple, only the working-age partner has 'work-related requirements'. See Chapter 6 for more on work-related requirements, and Chapter 7 for what happens if they are not met.

If the partner older than pension age is getting certain disability benefits, they are treated as having 'limited capability for work and work-related activity', which means an additional element can be included in the universal credit award and the claim will also include a 'work allowance'. These benefits are:

- attendance allowance
- pension age disability payment in Scotland
- the enhanced rate of the 'daily living component' of personal independence payment
- the enhanced rate of the daily living component of adult disability payment in Scotland
- the higher rate of the 'care component' of disability living allowance

If they are not getting any of these but are getting any other rate or component of personal independence payment, adult disability payment or disability living allowance, they are treated as having 'limited capability for work', which means no additional element of universal credit is paid but a work allowance is included in the claim.

For more on work allowances and extra elements of universal credit, see Chapter 5.

Are there other benefits for older people

As described above, many older people can claim **pension credit** instead of universal credit. Pension credit is a means-tested benefit which can include additional amounts for children, and for claimants who are severely disabled. In the future, it is intended that pension credit will also include amounts for rent, replacing pension-age housing benefit. However this is not expected to happen until at least 2028.

Universal credit does not replace state **pensions**. If you get a state pension and your partner is under pension age, you can get universal credit, but your pension reduces your universal credit pound for pound.

Attendance allowance, pension age disability payment and the **winter fuel payment** are not affected by universal credit and are not counted as income when working out how much universal credit you get.

7. People from abroad

Can people from abroad claim universal credit?

You can usually only get universal credit if you meet the 'immigration and residence conditions'.

Immigration conditions
The immigration conditions apply to people who are not British citizens.

You meet the immigration conditions for universal credit if you are (or, in some cases, are related to) a European Economic Area national and you have made a valid application to the European Union (EU) Settlement Scheme.

You can meet the conditions if you are a person from abroad and your immigration status means that you have 'recourse to public funds'. You have recourse to public funds if, for example, you are allowed to stay in the UK indefinitely without restrictions, or the UK government has recognised you as a refugee (but not while you are an asylum seeker), or you have been granted humanitarian protection or discretionary leave to enter or remain in the UK.

You do not meet the immigration conditions for universal credit if your entry clearance to the UK says you have 'no recourse to public funds'. This is usually stamped in your passport or on your biometric residence permit.

If you are unsure about how claiming universal credit might affect your immigration position, or want to apply to have the no recourse to public funds condition lifted, get specialist immigration advice.

Residence conditions
As well as satisfying the immigration conditions, you must generally also be 'habitually resident' in the UK in order to claim universal credit. This includes showing that you are settled in the UK and, usually, that you have been in the UK for at least one to three months. This condition applies to most people from abroad and also applies to British citizens returning to the UK from living abroad. It does not apply to refugees, those with discretionary leave to remain, and some other limited groups.

If you are a European Economic Area national with a pending EU Settlement Scheme application or 'pre-settled status' under that scheme, you must also have a 'right to reside' in the UK in order to claim universal credit. This requirement does not apply to those with 'settled status' under the EU Settlement Scheme.

> **What CPAG says**
>
> ### Right to reside
>
> 'Rights to reside' are complex. If you are currently working or self-employed in the UK, you are likely to have a right to reside, but there are also many other ways to have one. If you have applied for universal credit and been refused on the basis that you do not have a right to reside, get independent advice to check that this is correct. Your adviser can help you to ensure that the DWP has as much information and evidence as possible to determine your right to reside.
>
> If you are a European Economic Area national or relevant family member, do not have settled status or a right to reside, and do not have an alternative way of meeting the immigration and residence conditions, you are usually not entitled to universal credit. However, if you have pre-settled status and are destitute or at risk of becoming so, you may have entitlement to universal credit if you have a barrier to work. This is a complex area of welfare rights, so seek advice if you have been refused universal credit on the basis of not having a right to reside.

Are there other benefits for people from abroad?

There are special rules for people from abroad for most other benefits.

Further information

There is more information about the rules for current benefits in CPAG's *Welfare Benefits Handbook*.

There is more information about other kinds of financial assistance in CPAG's *Financial Help for Families: what you need to know*.

Appendix

Glossary of terms

Administrative penalty
A type of fine that can be offered to someone instead of being prosecuted, if the DWP thinks a benefit offence may have been committed.

Alternative payment arrangements
The discretion to pay universal credit twice a month, directly to a landlord or split between partners.

Appointee
Someone, usually a relative, who is authorised by the DWP to claim benefit on another person's behalf if that person cannot claim for themself – eg, perhaps because of a learning disability.

Assessment period
The monthly period on which universal credit payment is based. You are usually paid seven days after the end of each assessment period.

Bedroom tax
A reduction in the amount of the housing costs element for tenants of local authorities and housing associations who have a spare bedroom(s).

Benefit cap
The maximum amount of social security benefits that someone can receive. This includes most benefits, but there are some exceptions and some groups of people to whom the cap does not apply.

Budgeting advance
An advance payment of universal credit in the form of a loan, usually for people who have been on benefits for at least six months.

Capital
This includes savings, investments, certain lump-sum payments and property that is not a person's main home.

Care component
Part of disability living allowance and child disability payment paid if someone needs help looking after themself because of a disability or health problem.

Carer element
An extra amount of universal credit for people who care for a disabled adult or child.

Child element
An amount included in universal credit for someone responsible for a child.

Childcare costs element
An extra amount in universal credit for people in work who pay for childcare.

Civil penalty
A fine that can be imposed if someone is overpaid a benefit because they failed to provide information or gave incorrect information, and are not being prosecuted for fraud or another benefit offence.

Claimant commitment
A document setting out what someone must do while claiming universal credit, and the possible penalties if its terms are not met.

Conditionality
What claimants are required to do in return for their benefit.

Contributory benefit
A benefit for which entitlement depends on having paid a certain amount of national insurance contributions.

Couple
Two people living together who are married or civil partners, or living together as if they were a married couple.

Daily living component
Part of personal independence payment and adult disability payment paid if someone has problems with daily living activities.

Disabled child addition
An extra amount of universal credit for a child or young person who gets disability living allowance, child disability payment, personal independence payment or adult disability payment or who is blind.

Discretionary housing payment
A payment that can be made by a local authority to top up universal credit when someone needs extra help with their housing costs.

Earnings threshold
The amount of a person's earnings (or joint earnings for couples) above which there is no expectation to look for more work, or meet any other work-related requirements.

Elements
Amounts for children, disabilities, caring responsibilities, housing and childcare costs which make up part of a person's maximum universal credit award.

European Economic Area
The European Union member states, plus Iceland, Norway and Liechtenstein. For benefit purposes, Switzerland is also treated as part of the European Economic Area.

Flexible Support Fund
DWP payments that can help people get, or stay in, work.

Friend and family carer
A person who has taken responsibility for a child of a friend or family member under a formal caring arrangement, or under an informal caring arrangement if it is likely they would otherwise be looked after by the local authority.

Habitually resident
Someone who has a settled intention to stay in the UK, and who has usually been living here for a period.

Hardship payments
Loans of universal credit made if someone's entitlement has been reduced by a sanction and they face financial hardship.

Housing costs element
The amount of universal credit that helps with rent and certain service charges.

Independent Case Examiner
A body handling complaints about the DWP.

Judicial review
A way of challenging the decisions of government departments, local authorities and some tribunals against which there is no right of appeal.

Legacy benefits
The benefits that are being replaced by universal credit: income support, income-based jobseeker's allowance, income-related employment and support allowance, housing benefit, child tax credit and working tax credit.

Limited capability for work test
A test of whether a person's ability to work is limited by a health condition such that they are not expected to work.

Limited capability for work-related activity test
A test of whether a person's health problems are so severe as to limit their ability to prepare for work.

Limited capability for work element
An extra amount of universal credit paid to some people who are ill or disabled and who are not expected to work.

Limited capability for work-related activity element
An extra amount of universal credit paid to people who are too ill to prepare for work or who have a severe disability.

Main carer
The person in a couple who spends the most time looking after the children, jointly nominated by the couple. The law refers to the 'responsible carer'.

Managed migration
The term used by the DWP for the official process of transferring claimants to universal credit.

Mandatory reconsideration
The requirement to have a decision looked at again by the DWP before an appeal can be made.

Maximum universal credit
The amount of universal credit that someone is eligible for, before income is taken into account.

Means-tested benefit
A benefit that is only paid if someone's income and capital are low enough.

Minimum income floor
The amount of income a self-employed person is assumed to have, calculated by multiplying the national minimum wage by the number of hours they are expected to look for work.

National living wage
A set minimum hourly rate that employers must pay to people aged 25 or over.

National minimum wage
A set minimum hourly rate that employers must pay to people under 25.

Natural migration
The term used to describe the situation in which someone transfers to universal credit having decided to make a claim for it outside of the official managed migration process, usually following a change of circumstances for which they are unable to get the old means-tested benefits.

'New-style' employment and support allowance
A contributory form of employment and support allowance for those claiming under the universal credit system.

'New-style' jobseeker's allowance
A contributory form of jobseeker's allowance for those claiming under the universal credit system.

No recourse to public funds
A restriction that applies to some people subject to immigration control as part of their entry conditions to the UK, prohibiting them from claiming most benefits and tax credits, including universal credit.

Non-dependant
An adult, other than a partner, who lives with the person claiming benefit – eg, a grown-up daughter or son.

Non-means-tested benefit
A benefit that is paid regardless of the amount of someone's income or capital.

Overpayment
An amount of benefit that is paid which is more than a person's entitlement.

Passporting
A term used to describe when entitlement to a particular benefit allows access to other benefits or sources of help.

Pension age
This is age 66, and will reach 67 by October 2028.

Person subject to immigration control
Someone who requires leave to enter or remain in the UK but does not have it, or who has leave to remain but is prohibited from having recourse to public funds, or has leave to remain in the UK on the basis of a sponsorship agreement.

Qualifying young person
A dependent young person aged 16 to 19 in full-time non-advanced education.

Real-time information
A system where employers send HM Revenue and Customs information about employees' earnings every time they are paid, which is then used by the DWP to adjust universal credit awards.

Revision
A statutory method that allows benefit decisions to be changed.

Right to reside
A social security test, mainly affecting European Economic Area nationals, which must be satisfied in order to claim certain benefits.

Sanction
A reduction in a person's universal credit award for failing to meet their work-related requirements without a good reason or because they have committed an offence.

Sanction period
The length of time a sanction lasts for.

Severe disability premium
An extra amount in old means-tested benefits for someone who gets certain disability benefits, lives alone (or counts as living alone), and for whom no one gets carer's allowance.

Specified accommodation
Accommodation from a relevant body also providing care, support or supervision, or temporary accommodation provided because of domestic abuse.

Standard allowance
The basic amount of universal credit paid for a single adult or a couple.

Supersession
A statutory method which allows benefit decisions to be changed, usually as a result of a change in circumstances.

Taper
The rate at which a person's maximum universal credit reduces as their earnings increase.

Temporary accommodation
Certain types of homeless accommodation where payments are made to a local authority or a social housing provider.

Transitional element
An additional amount of universal credit for people who are moved to universal credit under the managed migration process and whose universal credit award would be less than their previous benefits.

Transitional protection
A way of making sure that a person being transferred to universal credit under the official managed migration process from another benefit will not receive less money on universal credit than they did before.

Transitional SDP element
A payment to compensate people who had a severe disability premium in their old benefit and have transferred to universal credit by 'natural migration' and have lost income as a result.

Two-child limit
A restriction on the number of child elements included in universal credit. There are exceptions – eg, if a child is adopted or for multiple births.

Universal credit advance
An advance of universal credit which can be paid if someone is in hardship while waiting for their first payment, if there is a delay in deciding someone's claim and in some other situations.

Universal support
Help to make or manage your claim and/or to budget.

Waiting period
The time before payment of certain elements can start.

Work allowance
The amount of earnings ignored before a person's universal credit award starts to be reduced. The amount depends on personal circumstances.

Work availability
One of the work-related requirements, which means being willing and able to take up paid work, usually immediately and within 90 minutes' travel time of home.

Work capability assessment
An assessment of whether someone has limited capability for work/work-related activity.

Work coach
Someone employed by the DWP to draw up claimant commitments, update them and check that claimants are meeting their work-related requirements.

Work-focused interview
One of the work-related requirements, which means attending an interview to discuss future work opportunities and the barriers to work.

Work preparation
One of the work-related requirements, which includes carrying out activities to prepare for a future return to work, such as increasing skills or doing a work placement.

Work-related requirements
The activities that a person must undertake to continue to receive the full amount of universal credit.

Work search
One of the work-related requirements, which means normally spending 35 hours a week looking for work.

Index

1
16/17 year olds, 22, 150
   entitlement to other benefits, 151

A
abroad
   going abroad, 26
   people from abroad, 26, 154
administration, 4
administrative penalty, 118
adoption
   two-child limit, 139
   work-related requirements, 105
adult disability payment in Scotland, 3, 149
   exempt from benefit cap, 76
advance payments
   budgeting advance, 42
   universal credit advance, 39
age rules, 21
   aged under 18, 22
   over pension age, 23
alternative payment arrangements, 40
   domestic abuse, 39
amount of benefit, 48
   benefit cap, 75
   calculating the amount, 68
   carer element, 54
   child element rates, 50
   childcare costs element, 59
   disabled child addition, 51
   hardship payments, 115
   housing costs element, 56
   income and capital, 63
   limited capability for work element, 52
   limited capability for work-related activity element, 52
   maximum amount, 49
   sick or disabled adult addition, 51
   standard allowance rates, 50
   transitional element, 73
   transitional severe disability premium element, 74
   work allowance, 64
amount of sanctions, 111
appeals, 128

appointees, 35
arrears
   payment in arrears, 38
   rent arrears, 42
assessment period, 4, 38
   employed earnings, 64
   two paydays in one assessment period, 65
asylum seekers, 155
attendance allowance, 3, 154
available for work, 96
   permitted exceptions to availability, 97

B
backdating, 36
bedroom tax, 57
   discretionary payment in Scotland, 57
bedrooms
   how many bedrooms are you allowed, 57
benefit cap, 75
   discretionary housing payment in Scotland, 57
   exemptions, 76
benefit offences
   hardship payments, 114
   prosecution for benefit offences, 118
   sanctions, 120
bereavement support payment, 3
   treatment as income, 66
Best Start foods, 3, 28, 138
Best Start grant, 3, 28, 137
budgeting
   help with budgeting, 40
budgeting advance, 42
   advance childcare costs, 61

C
calculation, 68
cancer treatment
   limited capability for work-related activity, 52
capital, 63
   capital limits, 28, 67
   income from capital, 67
care leavers, 22

Index

carer support payment in Scotland, 3, 144, 145
   exempt from benefit cap, 76
carer's allowance, 3, 144, 145
   exempt from benefit cap, 76
carers, 140
   carer element, 54, 140
   entitlement to other benefits, 145
   exempt from benefit cap, 76
   searching for work, 94
   work-related requirements, 103, 144
challenging a decision, 128
   overpayments, 123
   sanctions, 109
changes in circumstances, 44
   effect on award, 45
   failure to report, 117
   migration to universal credit, 14
   overpayments, 122
child benefit, 3
   treatment as income, 66
child disability payment in Scotland, 3
   exempt from benefit cap, 76
child element, 50
   two-child limit, 138
child maintenance payments
   treatment as income, 66
child tax credit
   replacement by universal credit, 2
   transferring to universal credit, 10
   transitional element, 73
childcare
   childcare costs element, 59
   deposits and advance payments, 61, 136
   evidence of costs, 61
   lone parents, 136
   looking after someone else's child, 103, 139
   preparing for work, 100
   reporting charges, 45
   searching for work, 94
   sharing care with former partner, 134
   work-focused interviews, 101
   work-related requirements, 104
childcare costs element, 136
children
   additions for disabled children, 51
   child element rates, 50
   hardship payments, 115
   looking after someone else's child, 103
   responsibility for a child, 50, 134
   three or more children, 138
   two-child limit, 50, 138
Citizens Advice, 4
   Help to Claim service, 32
civil penalties, 117
claimant commitment, 77
   accepting a commitment, 27, 79
   changing a commitment, 81, 86
   definition, 78
   failing to meet commitment, 107
   refusing to accept a commitment, 80
   work-related requirements, 82
claims, 30
   backdating, 36
   couples, 31
   how to claim, 32
   information needed to claim, 32
   problems claiming, 34
   reclaims, 35
   transferring to universal credit, 10
   when to claim, 36
   who can claim, 6
cold weather payment, 3, 28
complaints, 130
council tax reduction schemes, 28
couples, 19
   claims, 31
   definition, 19
   joint claims, 31
   joint earnings threshold, 90
   living together, 19
   mixed-age couples, 152
   older people, 152
   partner away from home, 31
   payment rules, 38

D
debts
   direct payments to creditors, 43
decisions, 35
   disagreeing with a decision, 128
deductions from benefits
   fines, 119
   hardship payments, 116
   overpayments, 126

Index

dental treatment, 29
Department for Work and Pensions, 4
  complaints, 130
disability living allowance, 3
  exempt from benefit cap, 76
  treatment as income, 66
disabled people, 146
  addition for disabled adult, 51
  addition for disabled child, 51
  additional bedroom required, 57
  carers, 140
  difficulties claiming, 146
  entitlement to other benefits, 149
  limited capability for work, 147
  preparation for work, 99
  searching for work, 92
  transitional protection, 15
  work allowance, 148
  work-related requirements, 105
  worse off on universal credit, 148
discretionary housing payment, 57
domestic abuse
  alternative payment arrangements, 39
  housing costs for two homes, 56
  refuge accommodation, 7
  work-related requirements, 106

E

earnings
  assessment period, 64
  calculating, 68
  changes in earnings, 44
  deductions from earnings to recover overpayments, 126
  earnings threshold, 89
  effect on amount of benefit, 63
  joint earnings threshold, 90
  two paydays in one assessment period, 65
  work allowance, 64
earnings threshold, 76
employed earners
  earnings threshold, 89
  effect of earnings on amount of benefit, 63
  joint earnings threshold, 90
employers
  reporting earnings, 64

employment and support allowance, contributory, 3, 149
  new-style employment and support allowance, 8, 9
  treatment as income, 66
employment and support allowance, income-related
  replacement by universal credit, 2
  transferring to universal credit, 10
  transitional element, 73
employment-injury assistance in Scotland, 3
entitlement
  basic rules, 21
  calculating, 69
EU Settlement Scheme, 26, 155
European Economic Area nationals, 154
  residence conditions, 155

F

Fair Start Scotland, 85
families
  payments for families, 49
  three or more children, 138
fares to hospital, 29
financial conditions, 28
financial help, 28
Find a job website, 87
fines, 117
  alternative to prosecution, 118
  amount of fines to avoid prosecution, 119
  payment, 119
  sanctions for being fined, 120
Flexible Support Fund, 61, 137
foster carers, 143
  work-focused interviews, 102
fraud
  civil penalties, 117
  prosecution for benefit offences, 118
free school lunches, 3, 29
funeral payments, 3, 28
funeral support payments, 3, 28

G

good reason
  avoiding sanctions, 110
guardian's allowance, 3
  exempt from benefit cap, 76

Index

H
habitual residence, 26, 155
hardship payments, 114
  amount of payments, 115
  applications, 115
  recovery of payments, 116
Healthy Start, 3, 28, 138
Help to Claim universal support service, 4, 32
HM Revenue and Customs, 4
home owners
  mortgage interest payments, 56
  service charges, 59
homelessness
  housing costs, 7
hospital patient
  limited capability for work, 52
hours of work, 4
  increasing your hours of work, 88
housing benefit
  accommodation covered by housing benefit, 7
  replacement by universal credit, 2
  transferring to universal credit, 10
  transitional element, 73
housing costs element, 56
  accommodation not covered, 56
  additional housing payments in Scotland, 57
  bedroom tax, 57
  non-dependants living with you, 58
  rent, 56
  service charges for owner-occupiers, 59

I
illness, 146
  addition for illness, 51
  hardship payments, 115
  preparation for work, 99
  searching for work, 92
  work-related requirements, 105
immigration conditions, 154
income, 66
  calculating, 68
  from capital, 67
  what counts as income, 63
income support
  replacement by universal credit, 2
  transferring to universal credit, 10
  transitional element, 73
in-work conditionality, 5
industrial injuries benefits, 3

J
Jobcentre Plus
  help finding work, 84
jobseeker's allowance, contribution-based, 3
  new-style jobseeker's allowance, 8, 9
  treatment as income, 66
jobseeker's allowance, income-based
  replacement by universal credit, 2
  transferring to universal credit, 10
  transitional element, 73
judicial review
  challenging a decision, 132

K
kinship carers, 143
  work-focused interviews, 102

L
legacy benefits, 2
legal aid, 29
limited capability for work, 51
  amounts of benefit, 52
  assessment, 53
  preparing for work, 99
  waiting for medical assessment, 93
  waiting period, 53
  work allowance, 63
limited capability for work-related activity, 51
  amounts of benefit, 52
  assessment, 53
  exempt from benefit cap, 76
  waiting period, 53
  work-related requirements, 105
living together, 19
loans, 42
  hardship payments, 114
local housing allowance, 58
lone parents, 134
  childcare costs, 59, 136
  entitlement to other benefits, 137
  preparing for work, 100
  searching for work, 94

Index

work-focused interviews, 101
work-related requirements, 104, 134
low income
    working extra hours, 88

M
maintenance
    treatment as income, 66
managed migration
    process, 12, 73
mandatory reconsideration, 128
maternity allowance, 3
    childcare costs element, 60
maternity leave
    work-related requirements, 104
maximum universal credit, 68
means-tested benefits
    replacement by universal credit, 2
medical examinations, 53, 147
    complaints, 131
migration to universal credit, 10
    managed migration, 12, 73
    natural migration, 14
minimum income floor, 66, 90
mistakes
    penalties for making mistake in claim, 117
mortgage interest payments, 56
MPs
    help from your MP, 131
multiple births
    two-child limit, 139

N
natural migration, 14
negligence
    penalties for negligent claims, 117
new-style employment and support allowance, 8
    claiming, 9
new-style jobseeker's allowance, 8
    claiming, 9
NHS health benefits, 3
no recourse to public funds, 26

O
occupational pensions
    treatment as income, 66

official error
    overpayments, 124
older people, 151
    entitlement to other benefits, 154
online claims, 4, 32
    changes in circumstances, 44
overpayments, 121
    challenging an overpayment, 123
    civil penalties, 117
    paying back an overpayment, 126
    reasons for overpayment, 122

P
parents
    childcare costs, 59
    preparing for work, 100
    searching for work, 94
    three or more children, 138
    without parental support, 22
    work-focused interviews, 101
    work-related requirements, 104
passporting, 29
payment, 38
    advance payment, 39
    alternative payment arrangements, 40
    Scottish choices, 41
    third-party payments, 43
    two paydays in one assessment period, 65
pension age, 23, 104
    mixed-age couples, 152
pension age disabilty payment in Scotland, 3
    exempt from benefit cap, 76
pension credit, 3, 8, 154
    couples, 23
person subject to immigration control, 26
personal independence payment, 3, 149
    exempt from benefit cap, 76
    treatment as income, 66
personal pensions
    treatment as income, 66
pregnancy, 104
    hardship payments, 115
preparing for work, 97
    illness or disability, 99
    parents of young children, 100
prescriptions, 29

prisoners, 20
private rented accommodation
  housing costs element, 58
public funds, 155

R
rape
  two-child limit, 139
recourse to public funds, 155
recovery of benefit
  hardship payments, 116
  overpayments, 126
reductions in benefits, 107
  bedroom tax reductions, 58
  daily rate of sanctions, 111
refugees, 27, 155
refuges, 7
religious orders
  fully maintained members, 20
rent, 56
  arrears, 42
  direct payment to landlord, 43
repayments
  hardship payments, 116
  overpayments, 126
replacement of benefits, 2
residence rules, 26, 154
residential rehabilitation
  limited capability for work, 52
retirement pension, 3, 154
  mixed-age couples, 152
  treatment as income, 66
right to reside, 26, 156

S
sanctions, 107
  benefit offences, 120
  challenging a sanction, 109
  daily rate of sanctions, 111
  ending a low or lowest level sanction, 113
  good reason for avoiding sanctions, 110
  hardship payments, 114
  length of sanctions, 112
  levels of sanctions, 108
  more than one sanction, 113
  when sanctions can be imposed, 107
savings, 67

school clothing grants, 29
Scottish child payment in Scotland, 3
Scottish choices, 41
searching for work, 87
  exemptions from searching for work, 94
  permitted restrictions on searching for work, 91
self-employed
  earnings threshold, 90
  effect of earnings on amount of benefit, 65
  minimum income floor, 66, 90
  reporting earnings, 44, 65
service charges
  owner-occupiers, 59
  tenants, 56
severe disability premium
  transitional protection, 15, 74
severely disabled person
  carers, 103
  limited capability for work, 147
  transferred to universal credit, 15
  work-related requirements, 105
sickness
  addition for sickness, 51
  preparation for work, 99
  searching for work, 92
  temporarily sick, 92
  work-related requirements, 105
sight tests, 29
specified accommodation, 7
standard allowance, 49
statutory adoption pay, 3
  childcare costs element, 60
  treatment as earnings, 63
statutory maternity pay, 3
  childcare costs element, 60
  treatment as earnings, 63
statutory paternity pay, 3
  childcare costs element, 60
  treatment as earnings, 63
statutory shared parental bereavement pay, 3
statutory shared parental pay, 3
  childcare costs element, 60
  treatment as earnings, 63
statutory sick pay, 3
  childcare costs element, 60

Index

treatment as earnings, 63
students, 23
   loans and grants, 66
   who can get universal credit, 24
   work-related requirements, 105
supported accommodation
   housing costs, 7
Sure Start maternity grants, 3, 28, 137

T
taper, 63
tax credits
   replacement by universal credit, 2
telephone claims, 35
temporary accommodation
   housing costs, 7
terminal illness
   limited capabilty for work-related activity, 52
third-party payments, 43
transfers to universal credit, 10, 73
transitional element, 73
transitional protection, 15, 73
   severe disability premium, 15
transitional SDP element, 16, 62
   amounts, 74
twins
   two-child limit, 139
two-child limit, 50, 138
   exceptions, 139

U
unemployment
   voluntary unemployment, 110
universal credit, 1
   amount of benefit, 48
   calculation, 68
   challenging decisions, 128
   claimant commitment, 77
   claiming, 30
   complaints, 130
   defining features, 4
   entitlement rules, 21
   financial conditions, 28
   introduction of benefit, 6
   overpayments, 121
   passporting to extra financial help, 29
   replacing means-tested benefits, 7
   sanctions, 107
   when can you claim, 6
   who can get universal credit, 18
   who cannot get universal credit, 20
   who has to claim universal credit, 10
   worse off on universal credit, 15
universal credit advance, 39

V
voluntary work
   availability for work, 97
   searching for work, 91

W
war widows, 3
   exempt from benefit cap, 76
widowed parent's allowance, 3
winter fuel payments, 3, 154
winter heating payment in Scotland, 3
work
   available for work, 96
   help finding work, 84
   increasing your hours of work, 88
   in-work conditionality, 5
   looking for work, 87
   preparing for work, 97
   searching for work, 87
   work-focused interviews, 100
work allowance, 64
   disabled people, 148
Work and Health Programme, 84
work capability assessment, 53
work coaches, 4, 84
work incentives, 5
work search requirement, 87
work-focused interviews, 100
work-related requirements, 82
   available for work, 96
   carers, 103, 144
   disabled people, 105
   domestic abuse, 106
   failing to meet requirements, 107
   illness, 105
   lone parents, 104, 134
   looking for work, 87
   no work-related requirements, 103
   over pension age, 104
   pregnancy, 104
   preparing for work, 97
   searching for work, 87

students, 105
waiting for medical assessment, 93
work-focused interviews, 100
working hours, 4
increasing your working hours, 88
working tax credit
replacement by universal credit, 2
transferring to universal credit, 10
transitional element, 73

Y
young people, 150
entitlement to other benefits, 151
qualifying young person, 50
single room in shared accommodation, 58